Commonsense Wisdom for Everyday Life

by

Joseph G. Langen

Sliding Otter Publications
Batavia, New York

Visit my web site at bccis.com/~jlangen.

Library of Congress Control Number: 2004093213

ISBN 0-9754928-0-2

Many of the topics in this book were previously published as columns in The Daily News, Batavia, NY.

Cover art by Peter Langen

Cover design by Susan Gagne

Printed in the United States by Morris Publishing
3212 East Highway 30
Kearney, NE 68847
1-800-650-7888

PREFACE

To me, wisdom is learning to look at ourselves, others, and the world in a meaningful way rather than mindlessly plodding ahead through life. Sometimes we think of wisdom in the abstract, not as a day to day help in living our lives. In this book, I offer you some bits of wisdom I have gathered from reading, meeting interesting people on my path and from my own inner experience.

Plato said, "The unexamined life is not worth living." The topics in this book invite you to look at what is going on in your life and in the lives of those around you. Hopefully these reflections will help you walk through your life a little more mindfully and stay focused on where you are heading.

I would like to thank Carol for bringing my spirit back to life and Gerry for his constant support now and in times of great turbulance in my life. Thank you to my mother for her unflagging belief in the goodness in all people. Thanks to my children and grandchildren who have brought joy to my life.

TABLE OF CONTENTS

CHAPTER 1

PERSONAL PERSPECTIVE

We all have our ways of looking at our own lives, each other and the world around us. Sometimes our views limit us or make our lives more complicated. Other perspectives sometimes serve us better. This is a chance to consider your outlook on life and decide whether you need to make any changes.

CHOOSING TO ENTERTAIN THOUGHTS

Ideas are running through our minds all the time. Some arise in the course of conversation, some through TV, radio or reading, and some just show up in our minds without invitation.

All sorts of ideas arrive everyday. Each idea has a message. War news may incline us to think the world is falling apart. Stories about arrests may lead us to think everyone is turning criminal. Criticism of others may encourage us to join in, finding fault with whoever is the topic of conversation. There are also positive ideas, but sometimes they tend to be overwhelmed by the negative ones.

We do have some control over what ideas end up in our minds. We can choose not to read or watch sensational news and not to associate with people who bombard us with criticism of everyone they know personally, as well as public figures.

There are times when we don't have control of our thoughts. We don't always know what will be in the news, what someone will say or what might pop into our heads without apparent provocation. Although we may not always have control of what thoughts come to our minds, we do have a say in how we respond to them. We may say to a thought, "Thanks for stopping by" and let it pass out of our minds as quickly as it entered. We may ask a thought to sit down for a cup of tea and entertain it for a while. We may also adopt a thought, make it our own, and introduce it to everyone we meet.

Our fears and prejudices, as well as the types of personalities we have, may make us more susceptible to negative thoughts, and may make it more likely we will entertain or adopt them. Still, there are things we can do. In addition to limiting the thoughts to which we expose ourselves, we have several other tools. We can be aware of the kinds of negative ideas which tend to sneak up on us and make a conscious effort to shoo them out the door rather than entertaining or adopting them. We can choose reading and TV shows which are likely to provide us with more constructive thoughts. We can be more judicious about the people we allow in our lives. If there are people we can't avoid, we can find a polite way to tell them we don't want to share their negativity.

Another way of focusing on the positive is a practice adopted by Henry David Throeau in the year he spent at Walden Pond. Each morning before getting out of bed, he wrote down things in his life that made him grateful that day.

While it is hard to change our personalities or ingrained tendencies, we can examine our fears and prejudices and work to eliminate them from our lives. All of this takes conscious effort, but is well worth it for our peace of mind.

THE MONOCLE

The New Yorker Magazine trademark popped out from the page the other day. A man holds up his monocle, a strange little lens dangling from a cord, to better focus on the world's details.The monocle, like other lenses, changes your normal view of things around you. When I did play therapy some years ago, I kept a variety of lenses in my office including binoculars, microscopes, magnifying glasses, and kaleidoscopes. My goal was to help children look at things in a different way than they were used to and later to start looking at their lives in a new way as well.

We all learn to see things in a certain way and tend to limit ourselves to our own point of view. The story of the blind men and the elephant demonstrates that we may have very different perceptions of the same thing if we experience only one aspect of it. What would you make of an elephant if you only encountered the tail, foot or trunk and not the rest of the animal?

Israelis and Palestinians have very different perceptions of their ongoing animosity. Opposing political parties differ in what they think is best for their nations, states and communities. Neighbors sometimes become passionate about seemingly small issues such as where clotheslines should be strung.

Strong opinions abound on all sides of all these issues, usually with everyone convinced they are right and the other side is bullheaded, stupid or just plain wrong.

No one usually wins such disagreements, and often everyone remains entrenched in their view, convinced they are right, accomplishing little in the controversy other than releasing a great deal of hot air and sometimes much worse. What if we had a mental lens which allowed us to see the point of view of those with whom we are locked in conflict?

The lens would allow us to set aside our convictions for the moment and listen dispassionately to what others may have to say. What is important to them? What do they really want? What if their wishes were not so different from our own? What if the other side also had a magic lens and could understand what it is like to have our convictions. Both sides could give each other a fair hearing.

Giving the other side a chance for expression may lead to seeing the similarities of seemingly contrasting views. What may initially look like very different positions may turn out to be different ways of saying the same thing.

With an open mind, we may also find out that the other

side has a legitimate point of view. What we hold dear may not be in anyone's best interest, including our own. We might find the best course is somewhere in the middle.

This is just an idea and would require a level of humility and openness most people do not usually feel when it comes to what is dear to them. But what if we tried it and found it worked?

TAKE TIME TO NOTICE THE LITTLE THINGS

My friend Judie has been watching a pair of nesting phoebes for several years. They build their nest in the most improbable space and tend their chicks with well coordinated teamwork. While driving along the expressway, Carol spotted a tiny fawn grazing along the median, seemingly oblivious of where its mother was, and added it to her gratitude list for the day. Driving on a back road, I noticed a row of cornflowers in front of a row of Queen Anne's Lace framing a cornfield in a subtle blue and white border.

None of these are earthshaking spectacles. They would all be easy to pass by without an awareness of the little things. It seems much easier for us to notice all the terrible things which bombard us each day and the worries which follow us around. If we let ourselves, we can become overwhelmed by all the awful things in life and collapse under their weight. Sometimes things which brighten our day take a special effort to notice.

Henry Thoreau wrote his memoir, *Walden*, in the nineteenth century. He described his practice of writing down the things for which he was grateful each day before getting out of bed. His habit was also suggested by Oprah as a way of keeping in touch with the good things in our lives. In order to list things for which we are grateful, we must pay attention to them and savor them as they happen. Some days it seems easy to generate a long list, and some days our troubles seem to block out the good things making them harder to remember.

The little things are usually subtle and, without practice, easy to overlook. Nevertheless, they are all around and waiting for us to notice them. The above examples are all from nature, but there are many other delights as well. A kind word, a loving gesture, or a small favor can all brighten our day if we let them.

The things we notice and choose to think about influence the kind of person we are inside and how we present ourselves to the rest of the world. If we constantly tune into tragedy, crime and conflict, we will undoubtedly become morose and negative about the world and eventually about ourselves. If we make an effort to notice the day's little gifts, we will have a brighter outlook on life despite our troubles.

Having a positive outlook can be contagious. A young woman I know, Megan, is so consistently cheerful, even when things are not going right for her, it is impossible to spend any time with her and not come away feeling more cheerful yourself.

We all have the choice of what to think about. We can

choose to descend into the doldrums or look for the joy in life. It might take some practice but we can brighten our lives and the lives of those around us as well.

FINDING YOUR INNER ARTIST

A newspaper recently featured articles recognizing the artistic creativity of Raymond Doward and Diana "DiDi" Martin.

Raymond started with natural musical and painting talent which he developed on his own. "I paint out of my emotions and out of my inner soul."

DiDi also started with talent but then had to struggle to regain use of her hand after an accident. "I realized God had given me a gift, taken it away and then graciously given it back again."

I still think of a painting my daughter did in second grade of colorful trees almost as if they were posing for a family portrait. I remember my son discovering his ability to conceive and produce metal sculpture at a time when he was close to hopelessness about his learning disability.

We are all born with the ability to notice our surroundings and interpret them in our own unique way. Did you ever listen to a child sing, or watch the drawings which emerge before lessons in the proper way to draw?

Many people think they have no talent and could not be creative if they tried. Once when I asked my son how he did his metal sculpture, he told me anybody could do it. I did not think this was quite true. However, I have thought about this many times and have reached the conclusion that everybody has a creative side.

With encouragement, some people develop their creativity and become famous or at least recognized for it. Others react to criticism and start to see their art as inferior, or worse, not really creative.

Mozart was able to write out a concerto in final form with no editing necessary. At the other extreme, some writers go through numerous revisions of their work before publishing it. Being creative does not necessarily mean the work is easy. Like childbirth, creative labor can be relatively easy or long and difficult.

Okay, what is art? One dictionary definition sees art as the "conscious use of skill and creative imagination." There are many kinds of art but they all seem to have in common imagination and a unique way of thinking about something.

Think about the mother who knows just what to say to a quite demanding child. How about the bank teller who brightens your day each time you enter the bank, even though you just went there to deal with money? Do you remember a coworker who helped you see a way to approach a problem which has been bothering you for some time?

Everyone has a unique set of life experiences which gives each of us a slightly different way of viewing life and its events. Your experience lets you see things in a way no one else can. This is the basis for your art. Whether it is sharing a way of doing things, decorating your house, choosing complementary clothes or even painting, sculpture, song or dance, you have an inner artist. Finding and letting your artist out can be very satisfying. Consider reading *The Artist's Way* by Julia Cameron.

PROSPERITY

Despite our stock market difficulties of late, we are still a wealthy country and most of our citizens are better off than they would be living in another country. What are we to do with this wealth and how should we think about it?

Some people see it as a contest, declaring, "He who has the most toys when he dies, wins." Some people hoard their wealth, worrying that they might lose it. Others think their wealth gives them the power to have their way with the world and gives our nation the right to dictate how we want the world to be.

Wealth and prosperity are often confused. Wealth means having money and things. The dictionary defines prosperity as the condition of being "successful or thriving." Having a great deal of money is not the same as being prosperous. Prosperity is not a measure of wealth but a state of mind. It means being comfortable with what we have, and being willing to share what we have with others.

It is easy to be jealous of those who seem better off than we are, wishing we had their wealth and privileges. It is easy to look down on others not so fortunate as we are, seeing them as lazy, unmotivated or a drain on the country's resources.

Once when I was walking by a very elegant house, I suddenly heard a great deal of screaming through its windows. One of the most intelligent people I have met was content to work as a lay brother in a monastery, cooking and sewing for others who had less talent than he possessed. The family was obviously not at peace. The lay brother was. It is not the amount of money we have which makes us prosperous. Nor would more or less money or things necessarily make us more or less satisfied with our lives.

What does make us prosperous? We can be thankful on a daily basis for what we do have. We can view what we have as passing through our lives rather than being ours. We can act as stewards of the money and things which pass our way and see ourselves as obligated to use what we have for the betterment of ourselves and the society we live in. We can pass on things or money we do not need to others who could make use of them.

At the time in my life when I first heard about the idea of prosperity, I was struggling to make ends meet and to satisfy my obligations. I decided that worrying about money or possessions would not increase them and decided to take a risk on prosperity. I have since found myself better off than I could ever have imagined. I am not the most wealthy person in the world, but I have learned to be satisfied with what I have and to share my good fortune with others. If you are interested in learning more about prosperity, you might consult the writings of Catherine Ponder or Eric Butterworth.

GETTING OLD ISN'T FOR SISSIES

Elke often found herself thinking about her situation these days. She was more likely to fall into reverie in the early morning hours before the sun came up. She wasn't so sure she liked her thoughts.

She was still quite independent. More so than most seventy-eight year olds could claim. She had her own home. She saw her friends. The few family members she had left visited her on a regular basis. She had always done her own shopping, did her own wash and was known for her elaborate meals.

Things had changed a few weeks ago. She landed on the floor, was aware of a tight feeling in her chest and found it hard to breathe. She later learned that she had a heart attack. This was quite a surprise to her. She took pains to exercise, if only to walk on a daily basis. Well, almost daily. She was usually careful about what she ate. She did not go to the doctor much, but then she did not have much call to go.

It wasn't that bad a heart attack, as such things go. Surgery was not suggested, although she was not sure what might happen when she was hooked up to all those tubes and wires. She didn't have to make many changes to her diet, but she did have to be more careful about salt. Just before leaving the hospital she started cardiac rehab.

She had always thought of exercise equipment as pretentious. Who needed a treadmill when there were sidewalks? Who needed a stationary bike when there were bicycles which took her somewhere and gave her a view of something besides a video display?

Her doctor explained that the equipment allowed better monitoring and control of her exertion. This was important to make sure she did not overdo it and cause more damage to her heart. It seemed they wanted to measure and control everything about her now. It was hard to accept. Well, maybe they knew what they were talking about. They were getting paid enough.

Elke stopped herself at that last thought. She said it out loud, "They were getting paid enough." It sounded a little sarcastic. She never thought of herself as sarcastic. Most of the people she knew who had a habit of being sarcastic were angry about something. Could she be angry?

She looked down at her fist and saw that it was clenched. Hmmm. As she opened her fist, she realized that clenching was not a usual activity for her due to the arthritis which had gotten a little worse in the last few years. What would she have to be angry about?

She thought again of all the things she still had: relative independence, a good mind, her cooking and sewing. Yes, they were all still there. She didn't like to think about what was missing. Her husband had been gone for a long time. She was ready to let go of him but her bed was sometimes cold, and maybe a little lonely. She had male friends but never thought of sharing her bed.

The heart attack was not the first time her body had let her down. The hysterectomy was more a bother than a loss. Cataracts clouded her world but the surgery made her see better than she had in years, despite having to get used to glasses. Gall bladder surgery meant she had to limit some of her favorite foods, but it was an incentive to eat healthier.

Elke had made the best of it except for the annoying arthritis which sometimes hurt and sometimes made small tasks quite difficult. Aspirin and swimming helped keep her arthritis at bay.

All in all, Elke thought she had always made the best of trying situations. If anything, she might be angry about her body asserting its mortality in such a dramatic way. If she thought about it, she would realize that the battle would eventually be lost, at least physically.

There was a time when she could not look beyond the mortal. When her husband died, she was comforted by an old friend, Jenny, who had also lost her husband. Jenny always seemed cheerful despite her loss. Elke finally asked her about her cheerfulness after puzzling over it for a while. Jenny explained that the way she looked at life was as a loan from God. Some people were loaned just a little life and some much more. This had helped Jenny understand what others referred to as dying too soon. It was not too soon, but just the end of the time God had loaned them. Jenny saw each day as precious and was glad to have another chance to see the sun come up. Elke gradually adopted Jenny's philosophy and also learned to accept each day on its own terms and on God's too for that matter. Still, getting old isn't for sissies.

CHAPTER 2

AGREEMENTS FOR LIFE

When we have considered our approach to life, we may decide to make some changes. We can start making agreements with ourselves about how we will proceed. Then we will be ready to change our contract with reality and move on to contracting with God.

BE IMPECCABLE WITH YOUR WORD

Impeccable is not a common word. Its use may refer to how someone is dressed, meaning there is nothing to quibble with. What does it mean for your word to be impeccable? The dictionary defines impeccable as "free from fault or blame" or "not capable of sinning or liable to sin." Sin is defined as "an offense against religious or moral law" or "an action that is felt to be highly reprehensible."

Being impeccable with your word is one of the agreements to be made with yourself from *The Four Agreements* by Don Miguel Ruiz. The above definitions are quite heavy duty. Are our words really all that important?

Remember the old saying, "Sticks and stones will break my bones, but names will never hurt me?" I have talked with a fair number of girls and women with eating disorders. One of the earliest memories almost all of them have is of family members making fun of how they looked. These early memories were the beginning, or at least part of the groundwork, of their eating disorders. Were you told things as a child which you took to heart and allowed to direct your feelings about yourself and your life choices?

Our words are important and tell others what we think and feel about them. Actually our words tell us how we think and feel about ourselves as well, and to some extent determine how we approach life. How we deal with situations may well depend on the label we give them. What we tell ourselves determines how we react to almost everything that happens in our lives. If something we don't like happens, we can tell ourselves it was either unfortunate or terrible. We can be sad or disappointed over an unfortunate incident but still go on with our lives. We can be stuck fretting for a long time over a terrible incident.

We can stir up trouble with our words. We can use our words to get back at someone who angers us. We can use what we say to make someone else look bad so we will feel better about ourselves. We can be careless with how we talk, making life more difficult for others without really trying. Or, we can be impeccable with our word and use what we say more constructively.

After considering the alternatives, being impeccable sounds like a better choice, but the whole idea sounds rather abstract. If we go around thinking about what we are about to say, how will we know if it is impeccable or not?

There is a simple way. When we have something to say, we can first ask ourselves if it is true, kind and purposeful. Have we observed it to be true or are we just making it up or repeating gossip? Will our words make someone else feel better? Will anything positive be accomplished by what we say? This approach takes some practice, but is important to how we live our lives and how others see us.

DON'T TAKE ANYTHING PERSONALLY

The second agreement presented by Don Miguel Ruiz is "Don't take anything personally." Even if you are impeccable with your word, not everyone else will be. Things people say can be quite hurtful, if you let them.

People do not express opinions for your benefit. They do it for themselves. If someone calls you stupid, they may be thinking they are smarter than you. They may wish you would do something so they would not have to. They may be angry that you have not learned to do what would make them happy.

People who call you lazy may wish they did not have to do so much work, may have high standards for everyone or may think you don't deserve to take a break.

People who call you clumsy might be inconvenienced by something you spill, may be embarrassed about people noticing the mess or may be clumsy themselves.

What about compliments? If people say you are pretty, handsome or ugly, does it make it so? It just means they feel good or bad when they look at you, but does not make you pretty, handsome or ugly, except in their eyes.

In each of the above cases, people's opinions are nothing more than them talking to themselves, sometimes out loud. What they say about us is not necessarily true. People say things for their own reasons.

This does not mean we should ignore what other people say. If we hear the same thing from everyone, it may be something to take into account. Still, all we know is that people may share a common opinion about us. Whether they are right or whether it makes any difference is up to us. If we like how others see us, there is no reason to change. If we don't like what we hear, we might want to think about what we can change. It is also possible we are not really the way people think we are. We might decide to change how we talk or how we act around others.

Living our lives is a personal choice, not a popularity contest. If we have thought about the meaning of our lives, considered what we want to accomplish while we are on earth and are going about doing what is important to us, others' opinions of us are not very important. This is especially true if we recall that their opinions are based on their own needs and wishes rather than on who we are.

If we try to keep everyone happy, we are doomed to failure. People often have contradictory expectations. Trying to be what everyone wants is like a juggling act which demands so much energy that we don't have the time to think about who we want to be. Listening to our inner voice keeps us focused consistently on our goals and helps others know who we are and what to expect of us.

DON'T MAKE ASSUMPTIONS

The third of the Four Agreements is, "Don't Make Assumptions." An assumption is "a statement accepted or supposed true without proof or demonstration." It is like having your feet firmly planted in midair.

What is so bad about assumptions? Let's consider an example which could also be used for taking things personally. Say a person bumps into you on the street. You assume the person is careless and get angry. You snap at him and tell him to watch where he is going. What if the person is blind, tripped over a crack in the sidewalk or saw something falling from a window above? You assumed the person was being deliberately careless while there are many other possible explanations for his behavior.

When we make assumptions, we create a fantasy world in which we imagine how things are and lose touch with reality. We are reacting to the world inside us rather than what is going on around us. Could our huge divorce rate be at least partly related to our listening to our own fantasies about our spouses, rather than taking the trouble to understand them?

When we make assumptions, we believe our thoughts are the truth. It is only our imagination, but we act as if it is real and end up making life more difficult for ourselves and for others. Our misinterpretations build walls where there could be relationships.

In addition to assumptions about others, we sometimes assume others know what we think and want. Have you ever gotten upset about a person buying you an ugly present for your birthday? You may think your friend knew what you liked and was trying to provoke you, when she may be under the impression that your taste is similar to hers. In this instance, both of you are acting under the mistaken assumption that your tastes are similar.

With assumptions like these, it is easy to take things personally when they may not have been intended that way at all. It might be interesting to know how many grudges are being carried around because of our fantasies and imagined affronts.

Not all of our assumptions have to do with other people. Sometimes we make assumptions about ourselves and our abilities. What if we think we are not very creative and give up on a dream we might have followed? What if Edison gave up on finding a way to make a successful light bulb after several hundred tries? We might also imagine we have abilities we really don't have and waste our time spinning our wheels.

What is the alternative to making assumptions? A motivational writer and speaker, Napoleon Hill, reacted to people's theories by asking, "What's the evidence for your opinion?" His answer was to find out the facts. Explore what is really going on behind your fantasy. Ask others what they mean when they say or do something, rather than assuming you know. Look for the evidence of our own abilities or shortcomings rather than jumping to conclusions. Freeing ourselves from false assumptions is a step toward being at peace with ourselves and with each other.

ALWAYS DO YOUR BEST

The fourth of the agreements is, "Always Do Your Best." When I first read this agreement, it seemed impossible. I thought of the times I felt I was doing my best: the oral examination for my doctorate, first learning to water ski, and the endurance test to qualify as a soccer referee. I was exhausted after each of these efforts and knew I could not stick with the pace for very long. How could I do this for any length of time?

I read further that doing my best means doing the best I can with the resources I have under the present circumstances. I discovered that my best varies from task to task. My best will be much better doing something I am proficient in than doing something I am just learning. My best will also be better when I am healthy, rested and focused than it is when I am sick, exhausted, or distracted. My best is not always the same but changes all the time. This made me feel a little better, and seemed a little more manageable.

I discovered that doing my best means pacing myself and not trying to do more than I can. Overexerting myself would quickly lead to exhaustion and either slow me down or prevent me from reaching my goal altogether.

I also learned that doing my best means actually doing something. Having good intentions is not enough. Telling myself I will get more exercise or eat better does not make me any healthier. It only makes a difference if I follow through on my intentions and do what I have been thinking about.

But it is not enough to take action. I can only do my best when I love what I am doing. If I am doing something just because someone else wants me to, or just because I will be paid for it or rewarded in some other way, it will probably not be my best. I have to be enthusiastic about what I am doing in order to use all my resources.

Doing my best also means accepting myself as I am, with the skills I have and with my level of functioning at the moment. Wishing I could do better distracts me from doing the best I can right now and only serves to discourage me by making me think how things could be under different circumstances.

This is not to say that I can't learn from my mistakes, improve my skills or find a way to change my circumstances so that next time my best can be better than it is right now.

I also need to remember that I am here to live, be happy, and love. If I keep focused on these three goals, I will be able to be the best me I can at each moment, with the abilities I have and under my current circumstances. I can live with that and rest easy when the time comes.

CHANGE YOUR CONTRACT
WITH REALITY

Does this idea sound strange to you? Isn't reality what it is, regardless of what you think about it. We have sayings in our culture for those we see as out of touch with reality. Get real! Get a life! Get with the program! Do we really need more dreamers in the world?

We tend to think reality is what we are taught about the world. Life isn't fair. You just can't get ahead. You have to take what you can get in life. We don't go around chanting slogans all day, but we might as well if they sum up what we believe about life.

Our first view of how the world works is from inside our family. We see how our parents, as well as older brothers and sisters, deal with the world. Did your father stay in a job he hated for thirty years? Were both your parents so busy working to support the family life-style that you hardly ever saw them? Did your dinner conversation focus mostly on other families' or your own misfortunes and frustrations?

Unless you have stopped to look at how you were raised, chances are you are probably living the same way your parents did. If you were lucky enough to have parents who took time to consider how they wanted their lives to be, you may have done the same thing and are now living harmoniously with those around you and with the rest of the world.

You may have come from a family which has dragged itself through generations of drudgery and you may be in no better shape than your parents or grandparents. Regardless of your heritage, you do have a choice of how to live.

Rather than accepting life in your old rut, you could choose to believe that your life can make the world a better place. You can do that by being aware of what others need from you. They may need someone to listen to how they feel, someone to offer them a compliment or just a kind word. You may also decide to change what you expect of others, what you expect of yourself or how you will deal with money and possessions.

A contract is a two way agreement. What will you get back from rewriting this contract? I have learned that you attract to yourself what you project. If you are angry all the time, you will attract anger from others. If you don't care about anything, you will receive indifference in return. However if you project caring for others, respect for yourself or a sense of prosperity, these same qualities will seek you out and surround you.

Rewriting your contract with reality is not necessarily easy. You can't just wake up tomorrow and be a whole new person. You can start to make some changes in how you think about yourself, others and the world and little by little adopt a new way of living which will change your relationship with the world and its inhabitants.

CONTRACTING WITH GOD

I was up in the middle of the night recently, with nothing better to do than see what was on television. I discovered a televangelist quoting every scripture passage he could find relating to prosperity. I listened while he explained that riches, a house, a better job and most anything else we would like in our lives was easily attainable by making a covenant or contract with God.

He went on to explain our part of the bargain which would insure God's largess. All we had to do was to call a number on the screen and arrange to send him one thousand dollars. It did not even have to be a lump sum, but could consist of payments. We could also contract to send him one thousand dollars each month, in exchange for his guarantee of whatever we wanted from God.

I had several questions. Who did he send money to if he wanted something from God? How did he get God to agree to have him promise whatever we wanted in exchange for one thousand dollars? How would he get God to deliver once he received our thousand dollars? Needless to say, I didn't send him a thousand dollars or even a down payment.

It seems to me this evangelist presumed to know and direct what God wanted us to do, and would do for us in return. It also happened to be to his benefit.

Although it might be nice to have a formula for what God wants of us, having it spelled out so clearly would take away the need for faith and trust in God. As it is, our lives are a quest to find out what skills we have as gifts from God. We also work to use them wisely in His service and for the benefit of our fellow human beings. Part of the challenge of our lives is unearthing and refining these gifts.

I have learned that prosperity has more to do with our attitudes about money, wealth, and possessions than it does with how we handle any particular amount of money. God hides treasures along our life path for us to find and use to our best advantage and to that of mankind as a whole.

Our contract with God does not have a dollar value on our part or a definite expectation of what God will give us in return. Our job is to use well what we are given. What we can expect from God is to be cared for in the way He/ She knows is best. This might not be in a way we expect but may consist of riches, earthly or spiritual, beyond our imagination.

I tend to be wary of others who say they know what is best for me, especially when they stand to benefit personally. In contrast, I enjoy traveling my life path with God, sharing what I have with God and others and being open to what is offered to me.

CHAPTER 3

SOCIAL RELATIONSHIPS

Once we have decided how to think about our lives, reached a contract with ourselves, with reality and with God, we are ready for our interactions with others. We have many choices of how to approach others. This chapter discusses some of the possibilities.

FAILED GREETINGS

The orange sun rays crept over the windowsill into my bedroom. By six-thirty, I was dressed and ready for a walk. Not a cloud in the sky, the early spring frost starting to be noticeable by its absence. Once I was off Main Street, there was no traffic. No one was about, although there were stirrings in some houses.

Starting to walk, I became more energetic and happier as the warmth of the sun opened my leather jacket. Squirrels dug and robins pecked for their breakfast. Buds burst on the trees. Shades of yellow and green began to emerge where last week bare branches reached out into the gloom.

Much as I relished the sun after a week of rain and clouds, I wished I had someone to share the day with.

I came to the tracks and remembered the photos I took last week of the rails curving in the woods. I congratulated myself for thinking to take these photos at exactly this time of day when the glint on the rails let them frame the emerging spring beauty of the woods.

Past the tracks was the ugly section of my walk. Old factory buildings and loading docks, all concrete, macadam and stone. A large truck backed up to the loading dock and a man stepped down from the truck. He started walking in my direction. Finally there was someone to share the day with.

"Good morning," said I in my most cheerful voice.

"..." was the reply.

He looked at me but made no motion with his eyebrows, eyes or lips. He played the Tar Baby to my Brer Rabbit. I knew immediately that it would not be worth pursuing him. Was he angry that no one was there to meet his truck? Did he need privacy to urinate in the woods? Did I interrupt his morning reverie? I guess I will never know. He left no clues as to his state of mind, intentions or needs.

Oh, well. It was still a beautiful morning. As I walked up Harvester Avenue and headed back down Main toward my house, I encountered a teenage girl. I thought I might say hello to her. She straddled the edge of the sidewalk closest to the curb and fixed her gaze toward the oncoming traffic as if expecting to find a friend. She studiously avoided eye contact with me and made it clear by her bearing that she had no interest in acknowledging my presence. It seemed that if I spoke to her she would yell for the police.

As we got closer, her gait stiffened. She used her peripheral vision to keep track of the sidewalk, keeping her eyes on the oncoming traffic. She managed to maintain her stiff bearing until we passed. I sensed her returning to her natural gait after we passed but did not turn around to see. Strike two.

As I continued down Main Street, I wondered whether I would have any more chances. In the distance I saw a figure slowly making its way toward me. As the distance closed, I made out a small person, a stooped adult, a woman. She shuffled along the sidewalk, taking on the challenge of each slab of concrete. She walked as if each section of sidewalk might suddenly break off and float to sea like an ice floe. As we got closer, I could see it took all her concentration to keep upright and moving forward. She kept her gaze fixed on the center of the sidewalk, as if daring it to move from her path.

Before I got within hailing distance, it was clear to me that this would not be the opportunity I was seeking. Her world consisted of herself and the sidewalk. I feared greeting her would break her concentration and perhaps bring her determined walk to an abrupt end. As we came still closer, my suspicions were confirmed and I could see her directing all of her energy toward maintaining forward progress. Not wanting to be responsible for a catastrophe, I chose to hold my peace and allow her to hold hers.

As she passed, I could see my house coming into view. No other pedestrians were in sight and it appeared unlikely that any would emerge from the few houses remaining between me and my destination.

With resignation, I climbed the porch steps, keeping my own counsel, as yet un-greeted by the world. Sitting down to breakfast, I consoled myself that surely someone at work would say hello. Maybe I should not wear my Nepal hat on tomorrow's walk. Maybe I should wear something besides my black leather jacket. Or maybe tomorrow the world would just be a little friendlier.

ONE SMALL KINDNESS

Imagine a day when everyone you met was kind to you, complimented you, or treated you with extra respect. Now imagine a day when nobody did any of the above. How would you feel at the end of each of these days? Now think about what you can do personally about world terrorism. How are these related? How can anything you do make a difference in the world, much less have an effect on something as monumental as terrorism? It is hard enough for our country to find a way to respond. Anything we can do as individuals seems puny by comparison.

Each of us comes in contact with a number of people during the day. These contacts are what we can control. We can influence people on the other side of our interactions in many ways. We can act impersonally- a business transaction with nothing personal involved. We can do our business and go our separate ways. At first, it appears we have contributed nothing to others. If they expect nothing of us, then doing nothing maintains a neutral balance. If they expect us to be friendly and we are neutral, we make their day a little worse. If they expect us to be hostile , we make their day a little better.

What if we go out of our way to be kind to others? What if we find something to compliment about them? What if we are just friendly and polite? How does this affect other people? If they have no expectation of us, they will be pleasantly surprised. If they expect the worst of us, they will be relieved. Even without speaking, a smile might also brighten their day.

This may seem like a lot of bother over one small interaction. If a toll booth attendant hands us a ticket and we thank him, so what? Big deal! But think of it this way. If everyone thanked the toll booth attendant all day, wouldn't he be more likely, on his way home, to treat the sales clerk more kindly on his visit to a store? If everyone who shopped with this clerk had an equally good day, wouldn't they be more likely to treat the clerk in a kindly way? How do you suppose the clerk will treat the next person with whom she comes in contact?

One small kindness is contagious. In itself, it may not be very powerful. However, the chain reaction you can imagine could have ripples around the world. In a concerted effort to show kindness to those we meet, we can have a cumulative effect down the line.

Our kindness toward others helps them be more understanding of what we are about. Their more positive response to us in return helps us take an interest in understanding them.

WATCH YOUR RIPPLES

With all the trouble and bad news in the world, people may wonder what the point is of being nice to each other. It often seems that over time society is becoming more callous and people are spending more of their energy meeting their own needs rather than looking out for each other.

While you may be able to get more money or things by putting yourself first at all costs, there is a price to pay. The price is that money and things become our only companions. We also let others know we care only for ourselves. By thinking only of our own needs, we teach others that we are to be avoided as a threat to their well being, since we are only interested in ourselves and not them.

I have heard many sermons over the years. One of the few which has stayed with me has helped set the course of my life. One Sunday morning many years ago, Father Brendan talked about our actions as being similar to a stone thrown in a pond. The stone creates ripples that travel far out and change the surface of the water for quite a distance. I have since heard of waves which travel all the way across the Pacific Ocean.

In a similar way, how we treat our neighbor is transferred to the next person and so on. Sometimes we discourage idealists who want to change the world. Even though none of us can recast the world to suit us, we can have a rippling effect on many people. Who knows how far the influence of our actions will carry?

Thought of this way, everything that happens between us and others has some effect on how the human race fares. If we do something negative, the world is a little worse off. If we do something positive, the world is a little better off.

I think it is easy to see our lives as insignificant among the billions of people inhabiting our planet. Our lives are quite brief in the context of the thousands of years of civilization. We tend to be aware of the momentous contributions some people have made during the course of history. Our small contributions may not make the history books, but may brighten the lives of those we meet and maybe countless others we have not met.

We do not often think of the effect our careless criticisms may have. Likewise, we may not be aware of the positive effect we have through our kindness toward others, and how far the effect may travel.

Our mission, should we choose to accept it, can be to leave the world and its inhabitants a little better off than we found them. Rather than selfishly looking only after own needs, or being critical of others, we can care for others in little ways. The ripples of our actions can travel far and wide, eventually returning to enhance our own lives.

BEING PART OF THE STORY

Each of us is the central character in our own lives. Minor characters come and go, supporting characters remain in the background and antagonists challenge us. However each of us stays squarely in the middle of our own story. We tend to take our central place for granted since we are most familiar with our own lives. We have our joys, sorrows and tribulations to face each day, and tend to be preoccupied with them.

At the end of the day, we might think of the choices we have made since morning. We are happy when our decisions work out well and sad, angry or disappointed when they don't. We are glad to encounter some of the people in our lives, take some of them for granted, and studiously avoid others. It is as if the world revolves around us, other people forming the background of our lives.

While it seems there are people moving in and out of our lives constantly, it is only true from our perspective. From our point of view, our lives are constant while the cast of characters, other than ourselves, enters and exits our stage. Did you ever stop to think what it is like from the perspective of the characters in our own little drama? Each of them has their own ongoing play while they see us as minor characters moving across their stages.

If we think only of our own lives, it is easy to expect the minor characters in our lives to play the role we want them to play. It is as if our drama is the only important one. Would we live our lives any differently if we stopped to consider that each person passing through our lives is also in the middle of their own drama? Each one is just as concerned with their own story as we are about ours.

When we meet people, the first two questions are usually their names and what they do for a living. What if we asked how each person who passes through our lives, no matter how briefly, could enhance our lives and how we could enhance theirs? Sometimes prejudices encourage us to write off certain people before giving them, or ourselves, a chance to benefit from touching each others' lives.

Even people we see as toxic can leave us with something positive. Without allowing ourselves to be injected by their poison, we can use the experience to our advantage. Are there any ways in which we are being toxic, or detrimental, to other people's attempts to live the best lives they can?

Fortunately, most of the people we meet are not toxic. They are in search of ways to better themselves, at least at some level. There are two questions we can ask ourselves as each person walks across our stage. Does this person know anything that could help us improve our life? Have we learned anything in our lives that could help this person improve his or her life?

TAKE TIME TO LISTEN
TO A FRIEND IN NEED

When asked about friendships, we usually think of the good times with our friends. We recall outings, celebrations or just sitting around enjoying each other's company. Friends are the ones we call in good times and who comfort us in bad times. They consist of our spouses, relatives, childhood chums, and people we have met through work, sports or community activities. There are various degrees to which we share our hopes, dreams, fears and disappointments, depending on the closeness of the friendship.

While it is easy to think about what we get from friends, sometimes it is harder to think about what we give back. The good times are easy. It is a joy to be with our friends, basking in the reflection of their good fortune, when they are on top of the world. Although harder, we can rise to the occasion when our friends are in crisis through illness, death of a family member or other misfortune.

Friends can also have long term difficulties which may test the bonds of our friendship. Our friends can develop a pattern of long term depression, debilitating chronic illness, marital problems or financial difficulties. I think the greatest challenge is when our friends become mired in long term struggles, with no end in sight. There is no quick fix; nothing we can do results in an easy solution. What can we do? What would our friends like from us?

A while back, there was some research on what people want from friendships. Money, advice and problem solving were not what people desired most from a friendship. What did rank high were listening and understanding. Most people want their friends to hear and understand what they are going through.

Even if you could solve someone else's difficulties, how helpful would that be? The immediate problem might be solved, but your friend would not learn what to do the next time this situation arises. Having someone else solve our problems may leave them feeling dependent and helpless.

How do listening and understanding help? Do you remember that last time you were stuck with a long term difficulty? Probably the worst thing about such a situation is feeling all alone. We may feel ashamed of getting ourselves into a pickle, hopeless about ever resolving it or abandoned by everyone around us.

Through listening and understanding, we can show we are still there no matter how bad things get. We can let our friends know they are still loved regardless of their circumstances. Even if they have caused their own hardships, our continued understanding and support can show we believe in their ability to work things out.

In some ways it is like being a cheerleader. It is difficult to be enthusiastic about cheering when your team is behind, but that is when we are needed most. Seeing our friends through the tough times will make our friendships all the more enjoyable once the difficulties are resolved.

LISTEN TO THE BUTS

Have you ever noticed that in conversation, most people will agree with you to a point? Then they will throw in a "but" at the end of their reply, which tells you they don't really agree with you. "I like your shirt, but the color clashes with your pants." "Karen is quite friendly, but might be just trying to impress people." "George can be quite helpful, but there is usually something he wants in return."

We often hear the agreement in the first part of the reply, and feel we are on the same page. We might miss the "but" at the end, signaling that we are not as close together in our thinking as we would like to be. Part of the reason we miss this subtlety is our greater interest in getting our point across than in hearing what others have to say. Sometimes people agree with us just to be polite. Sometimes people will just let us keep talking unless we make a point to ask what they think.

Some writings on social conversation suggest that it is not important to have anything to say in order to be viewed as a good conversationalist. As long as we listen and make people feel understood, they will walk away from us feeling they had a good conversation, even though we may not have volunteered anything about ourselves or our opinions.

A study in the 1970's of what people thought made a good friendship did not see advice, knowledge or experience with their problems as highly important. What was most important to most people was feeling understood. I think we too often focus on what we can do for our friends, rather than on leaving them with the impression that we understand their feelings and point of view. We want to take over rather than just listen.

When others express partial agreement with us, followed by a "but," we are more likely to find out what they really think by listening closely to what follows the "but." The second half of their statement may be expressed quietly while we go on explaining what we think. We may miss altogether that there is something else to be considered besides our own point of view.

How do we go about finding out what someone else thinks? Some people like to argue and will state their point of view quite plainly. Other people may be too polite to interrupt or contradict us and leave us with a weak little "but" or perhaps a glance or tone of voice, giving us a hint that there may be other opinions brewing besides our own.

If we truly care what others think, we can pick up on the "but" and let them know we heard their opinion and that it differed from our own. We can also respond to their expression or tone of voice and ask them to tell us what they think.

It is gratifying to know that others understand what we are saying. It is much more satisfying to know what others think as well. Our clarification of the other side may also help us avoid misunderstandings in the future.

ARE YOU SURE YOU
WANT TO JUDGE PEOPLE?

By the time we are adults, most of us reach some conclusions about how we should live our lives. We have a sense of what is important to us, what is right and wrong, as well as the best way to do things. We could sum up these approaches to life as our set of values. We develop these values from our family traditions, our personal experiences and our learning, formal and informal.

Once we have developed our values and learned to live by them, there is a tendency to use our values as a standard for rating others' behavior. Do they meet the expectations we set for ourselves? Do they do things the way we would? Do they have the same priorities we do?

We tend to forget that others may not have had the same life experiences we did. They may have learned to view the world, and themselves, in very different ways than we have. Expecting others to think like we do often causes difficulty in close relationships such as marriage.

Cultures often have values, beliefs and rituals which would be abhorrent to members of another culture. Circumcision, extensive tattoos, and puberty rites are all seen as essential in some cultures and barbaric in others. A variety of religions view themselves as the one true religion with all others as misguided at best. Throughout history, wars and persecutions have abounded in the name of belief in one true religion. Much of the unrest in the Middle East is motivated by conflicts between religious and cultural beliefs. Does it make sense to kill each other in God's name?

I am not suggesting that most people go around killing others with different beliefs. I do think it is fair to say that most of us have a tendency to apply our standards to others and to judge them accordingly. However there are a variety of ways we can react to the differences we find between ourselves and others.

We can condemn or ridicule others to their face and in public in an attempt to shame them into thinking the way we do. We can ask them about their beliefs, seeking an understanding of why they think and act the way they do. We can also assume they are doing the best they can with the skills and knowledge they have at their disposal.

We don't have to agree with what others do, accept their priorities in life or have the same beliefs they do. But we don't have to expect everyone to be a carbon copy of ourselves either. No one else has had the same experiences we have. Even people growing up in the same family can turn out very different.

Giving others the benefit of the doubt can make our interactions more pleasant for all concerned. Approaching others with openness rather than hostility makes it more likely people will understand each other. In this way it is easy for us to find common ground rather than fighting to make everyone else like us.

THE ANGELS AMONG US

Sometimes when we pick up a newspaper or turn on a TV news program, it seems quite a task to find something positive about anyone. The world seems populated by murderers, abusers, thieves and other ne'er-do-wells. In our casual conversations, the topic is often, "Did you hear about so-and-so?" We almost seem to be waiting for bad news.

I recently found myself in St. Joseph's Cathedral in Buffalo watching eighty two people receive the St. Joseph Award from their Bishop for outstanding service to their parish communities. I did not know eighty one of the people who received awards, but I did know one and have seen some of his contributions to his family and community over the last six years. I would imagine that each of the other eighty one have made contributions on a par with those of the one person I know.

Many of the people we hear or see singled out in the news for their evil deeds came from troubled backgrounds and have used their history as an excuse for their disruption of society. The man I know came from a difficult family background as well and would have had an excuse to leave others to care for themselves or concentrate on meeting his own needs. However, he somehow overcame his up-bringing and has left behind any tendencies to be stuck in his early experiences. I have never met anyone more de-voted to his wife and children, going out of his way to meet their needs despite any illness or exhaustion on his part, not to mention mere inconvenience. He is also avail-able to relatives and friends whenever he can be of help. His award was for the same level of selfless service to the members of his parish. His sister sees him as nothing short of a miracle, and I have to agree.

There are evil people among us. However there are cer-tainly Angels walking among us as well, touching the lives of many people. I am sure that if you stop to think about it, your life has been touched by at least one.

These angels also wrestle with health, bills, and all the same life stresses the rest of us face. Rather than being dragged down by life's challenges, each one of them seems to be refined like smelted gold by life's challenges and is able to rise above the past to become a valuable asset and example for the rest of us.

How this happens is a mystery or, considered another way, a miracle. We are all blessed to have miracles taking place around us and to have our lives touched by these human Angels in our midst, although we may sometimes take them for granted. Next time you experience a miracle or are touched by the Angels in your life, let them know you appreciate their making your life a little better.

CHAPTER 4

PROBLEM RELATIONSHIPS

Sometimes relationships become troublesome despite our best efforts. People do not always make it easy for us to get along with them. Here are some ways to deal with people who aren't so easy to to reach.

DON'T BE AFRAID TO LOVE

"What good is sitting alone in your room?" asks the song from Cabaret. On the surface of it, being alone, especially in a lonely way is not a happy prospect. Being alone and being lonely are not the same thing. It is good to be comfortable with your own company. Too much time alone, though, leads to isolation and loneliness for most of us. We are social creatures and are made to spend time with other people.

Research suggests that normal development for babies depends on close, intimate, comforting contact. Development through childhood and adolescence into independent adulthood also depends on emotional support. Having others around who frequently remind us of our value helps us learn that we are worthwhile and that we can trust our own judgment.

We also learn to be comfortable in relationships through the support we receive from family and friends while we are growing up. Unfortunately, not everyone has the advantage of this kind of emotional support.

Imagine being told on a regular basis that you were a bad child. Imagine being ignored by your parents, who always seemed to have better things to do than to be bothered paying attention to you. You would most likely end up feeling you were not very worthwhile as a person and would probably not know you had anything to contribute to another person in a relationship.

Even if you were raised in a loving family, how would you feel if you were betrayed by your spouse or partner? In this case, it would be harder for you to love again. I have heard marriage described as learning to live comfortably on a powder keg. Things can blow up at any moment. Love has no guarantee. Even a faithful spouse can become ill or die.

While bad outcomes are always possible, there are ways we can maximize our chances of maintaining a loving relationship. Looking out for our own needs first, not getting too close in order not to be hurt and trying to control the relationship are all ways of making things worse. Not surprisingly, the opposite of these three approaches may give us the best chance of maintaining a loving relationship.

Putting the needs of your partner before yours makes it clear the relationship is important to you. Taking risks in a relationship, such as talking about your insecurities, is a way of showing your trust of your partner. Sharing control of what happens in your relationship or sometimes deferring to your partner are ways of avoiding power struggles.

Being afraid to try any of these approaches can keep us on the sidelines without much chance of maintaining a relationship. Since there is no rule book for relationships, the best approach is to be open to taking chances and to talking about what the relationship means to each other. We can also be humble when our efforts do not have the effect we expect, and be ready to forgive when our partner's efforts fall short.

WHAT ARE YOU DOING IN MY LIFE?

When things are going well, we enjoy sharing our good fortune with those who care about us. When we go through hard times, we appreciate having friends to support us. Sometimes people seem to turn up in our lives and stay involved but are of no particular benefit to us or whose destructive influences far outweigh the benefit of having them around.

Who are these people? Where did they come from? What can you do about them? The first challenge is recognizing them. Some people are rather harmless but don't contribute anything. They don't rejoice at your success, understand your hard times or help make your life better.

Somehow these people became part of your life. You

weren't born with them around, except those who are relatives. You didn't invite them into your life, at least not to act the way they do. You would like them to be less a part of your life but they always seem to be there.

Some of these people were not always this way. I remember a woman I loved as a child. She took me everywhere and doted on me. I called her my aunt although she was just a neighbor. I had not seen her for many years and was excited about seeing her at a funeral we would both be attending. Some of my relatives gave me a strange look when I said I was looking forward to seeing her again. It is hard to find words to describe what she had turned into. Her face was contorted in a permanent scowl, her voice perpetually shrill and her comments consistently negative and critical. Certainly it wasn't what I expected.

These are a few examples of the toxic people you wish were not quite so prominent in your life. Wishing does not usually change anything. What can you do to get your life back?

Fortunately, there are three options. One is the direct approach. Work for a different kind of relationship. No one likes to be criticized. Start by letting the other person know what things you like about your relationship. Hopefully, there are some. Gently say what behavior of theirs annoys you and why. Notice, you don't tell them what they are doing wrong. You are talking about your feelings about how they act.

Another option is to cut off your association entirely. This is an unpleasant and drastic step. Sometimes it is necessary if you just can't get the other person to appreciate your annoyance or get anything to change. This is also

harder to do if the person is a relative or even a relationship partner, but sometimes it is necessary to preserve your
sanity.

Perhaps the best approach is to avoid getting entangled
with such people in the first place. This is difficult if they
change after you have known them for a while. Understanding your needs and wishes regarding a relationship
and being careful to get close only to people with whom
you are compatible can save you a great deal of annoyance and conflict later on.

SOMETIMES YOU HAVE TO LIMIT FRIENDSHIPS

I once wrote about extending ourselves to friends in need
and how to be helpful to them. As I wrote, I was aware
that friendships can sometimes go only so far. There may
be times when it is better to back off.

Some assumptions I made were that friendships are mutual and that we should get a response to our efforts to
help. If we are doing all the giving and get nothing back,
we are being caretakers rather than friends. If our efforts
go unnoticed or are resented, we may be wasting our time
or annoying someone we thought we were helping.

Sometimes friends do not want our help. They may prefer
to solve problems at their own pace or in their own way
without our input. They may find our suggestions confusing or overwhelming. Sometimes people are not ready to
change their lives and may feel rushed by our efforts to

help. A friend struggling with alcohol may feel that drinking is still more comforting than damaging and may resent what they see as our interference. Trying harder to help might just increase the friction between us and them.

Insisting on being helpful when our input is not wanted may further damage our friendships. Our fruitless efforts may eventually draw us into our friends' difficulties without our being able to contribute anything. We may end up spending more time and effort fretting about their problems than they do.

Sometimes friends tell us bluntly when our help is not wanted, saying their problems are none of our business. The message can be more subtle. Our attempts to help may be acknowledged, but our friends may continue their self destructive behavior. Sometimes it is hard to tell when our efforts are appreciated or wanted. It's not a bad idea to ask our friends if they would like our help with a particular problem or would appreciate our listening to their struggles.

If our efforts to help reach an impasse, we have several choices. We might tell our friends we would like to be helpful but realize they would like to tackle the problem on their own. We might check in with them from time to time to see how they are doing and ask them to let us know if we can be of help in the future. The most drastic step is to end our friendship. It is hard to conclude that a friendship might be damaging to us. There are times when this might be the only possible conclusion. If a friend continues to choose a criminal life-style, to wallow in addiction rather than seeking help, or blames us for problems they have created, it may be time to step back from the friendship for a while or even permanently. We don't want to be like the boy scout who came home with a rumpled and torn uniform. When asked what happened, he explained, "I tried to help a lady cross the street, but she didn't want to go."

SOMETIMES WE COMMUNICATE TOO WELL

When people seek marriage counseling, they typically start by saying they have a communication problem. They proceed to elaborate on what is wrong with each other. "If you would only change, everything would be fine." "You never listen to me." Then they continue to argue about who should change, both insisting it is the other one who is at fault for most of the problems in the relationship.

One thing I have noticed about this exchange is that couples usually understand perfectly well what each other are saying and can quote each other word for word. What couples really mean is that they don't like what they are hearing from each other. The problem is in the words exchanged, but it is not a question of misunderstanding. It is a matter of hurtful words being hurled at each other. To be more accurate, couples should say they don't like what is being communicated.

How do things get to this point? If couples talked this way to each other at the beginning of their relationship, there would not be a second date. No one would have an interest in continuing to spend time with someone who is nasty and critical.I think there are at least two factors which lead to deterioration in a relationship. The first is assumptions. People sometimes assume they know how their spouse thinks. They also assume their spouse understands how they think. Both assumptions may be correct, but it is equally likely they are false. Unless we clarify our assumptions we may be expecting things of each other which have no basis in reality. Even if our assumptions were correct at the beginning, we change over time. What we think now might be radically different from what we once thought. Our assumptions may have been correct once, but eventually may become outdated.

The other factor is our choice of pronouns when we talk to each other. Consider the difference between these two sentences. "You never consider my needs." " I would like to spend one evening a week with you and without the children." The first is an accusation and an attack which usually leads to the other spouse becoming defensive or attacking back. The second sentence is a clear statement of needs and invites a discussion and planning rather than an argument.

Our communication becomes a problem when we use it to blame each other for how we feel. We tell our spouse it is all their fault that we are sad, angry, or whatever else we feel. We do not take any responsibility for our feelings and do not tell our spouse what we need or want. No wonder we end up in arguments.

By being clear about what we and our spouses want, we have a much better chance of meeting needs on both sides and maintaining a more peaceful relationship. Then we have a much better chance of maintaining good commmunication.

IS IT TIME TO LEAVE MY MARRIAGE?

This is a very difficult question for anyone who has been married for any length of time. I would dare say that most people who marry "Until death do us part," mean it and have no intention of dissolving their marriages. Yet, in recent years, there has been one divorce for every two marriages in our country. Even in religions which do not believe in divorce, such as Catholicism, there are estimates of 50,000 annulments compared to 300,000 marriages per year.

I think many of these failed marriages result from not answering a much earlier question, "Is it time for me to get married." Many people marry for reasons such as sexual needs, companionship or economic security without really getting to know themselves or their potential spouse. We often do not stop to think whether we are ready to make the sacrifices necessary to help a spouse reach his or her life goals. Can we compromise with our own goals in order to work together? Do we even know what our own and our spouse's goals are? If we can't answer these questions, it is probably not time to get married.

Even if we have agreed on mutual goals, things change. Most marriage vows include the phrases, "for better or worse," and "in sickness and in health." In wedding rehearsals, my uncle, who was a priest, used to add "for thinner or fatter." When we marry, we do not spend our wedding day thinking of all the things that can happen to us in the future.

How is it that some couples seem to weather almost in-surmountable odds while others watch their marriages crumble for seemingly insignificant reasons? When you ask a couple in trouble with their marriage what happened, they usually admit they can't communicate. Since people are always changing, we need to talk about the changes in order to adjust our relationships accordingly. Otherwise we may find ourselves increasingly at odds as we go along. It is necessary for both spouses to remain open to under-standing each other and to accommodate to each other's changing needs. A one sided marriage usually does not last.

Since communication is an issue, it is often difficult for troubled spouses to resolve their own problems. They usually need to get help from an understanding counselor or clergyman. One spouse may decide their own needs are more important than those of their spouse and be closed to compromise. If you are married to such a person who will not change, even with help, it may be time to recon-sider the marriage. The person with whom you agreed to share your life may have become toxic to you, and under-mine your efforts to live a good life rather than working with you to make your life worthwhile.

This is a difficult conclusion to reach and one not arrived at lightly. If all efforts to mend the marriage fail, you may face a choice of living in mutual misery or moving on to separate lives. This is a scary prospect after many years of marriage, but may be necessary for your well being.

CHAPTER 5

FAMILY RELATIONSHIPS

Some of the most complex relationships exist among family members. Unlike other social relationships, we don't get to choose our parents or our children. They are also not so easy to leave behind when things do not go well. Following are some thoughts on the family and some ways to manage family issues.

THE NATURE OF FAMILIES

Today's families are under a great deal of tension and can congratulate themselves if they are able to stay together. There are a number of tensions from the times we live in and other tensions from changes taking place in the family. Money is something most families struggle with from time to time. Many parents grew up to feel that having enough money, or at least enough credit, was one of their rights. As inflation has made more money necessary to keep pace, families have felt pressure to find more money, leading to many more second jobs as well as two worker families. These trends have made it harder to raise children so that it is rare for either parent to be able to just raise children and not work outside the home.

The moving of families has changed the old ways of growing up in the same neighborhood with cousins, aunts and uncles and grandparents. Children often move several times while growing up, sometimes to far away cities with no family around. Family customs tend to get lost, or at least fade, as people see less of their relatives.

Also, the "Me Generation" shows little sign of going away. Looking out for number one may have something to do with money and moving. Whatever the reason for it, when two people who have grown up thinking about themselves first get married, it is hard to put aside their own needs and wants and think about what is best for a spouse and children. While in the past people saw marriage as meant for raising a family, good birth control has made it possible to marry without even thinking about children.

There are a number of normal changes which take place in families that can tax their strength. Adding a child to a family means changes in how the family is set up and in what family members need from each other. Losing a family member who leaves home or dies makes it harder on those remaining in the family.

Each member leaving a family has a role to play which must be taken on by other family members. If this role is not taken on, the family can feel confused or incomplete without always knowing why. Tensions not found in all families can be even harder to tackle. It is hard to act normally when one member of the family is sick, drinking or on drugs, learning disabled or for some other reason is not able to carry on as usual in the family. The whole family setup may change through separation or divorce, sometimes leaving one parent to act as a single parent and the other becoming a visitor.

If all tensions came about in the family in the same way, they would be easier to handle. Unfortunately this is not the case. Some tensions start within the family such as learning that a child has a hearing impairment. Others start outside the family such as one parent losing a job. Some tensions bother all members of the family such as a divorce while others bother only one member such as a child's problems with a teacher. Tensions can be sudden such as the house burning down or gradual as in the growing up of a teenager. Tensions can be strong as in the death of a family member or mild as in having a small car accident. The effects can be long lasting as in remarriage of one parent or fairly short such as with a broken leg. Tensions can be expected as when a grandparent gets older and needs more care or unexpected such as with a hurricane. Nature can be the cause such as in a flood or people can be the cause such as when a family decides to move. Finally some families seem to handle tensions while others seem out of control.

All of these affect how the family thinks about itself and what is happening to it and will have something to do with how the family acts under pressure. Also the family's response to tension will usually depend on what has been learned from grandparents and on how well the family has handled past tensions.

STAGES OF FAMILY GROWTH

Some people think a family is a family and that their family is the same now as it was five or ten years ago. This is about as true as saying that a fifteen year old is the same as he or she was at five or ten. Sometimes it is easier to see changes in a person than it is to see them in a family. But just as a person grows and changes, a family changes over time and hopefully matures. A number of stages can be seen in most families as talked about by Jay Haley in his book, *Uncommon Therapy*.

The first stage is courtship, when two people think about getting together to start a family. Animals have many courtship rituals and ways of choosing mates. Humans are the only ones who can take on any of these ways, from casual mating without staying together to lifetime partnership. Humans are also the only species to have in-laws. Older generations in most animal species have little or nothing to do with finding a mate, childbirth or raising the young. In the human species, relatives can be highly involved in all stages of family life. Some marriages take place in order to get away from parents. If this is the main reason for the marriage, once the escape is made, there may be no further reason for the marriage and tension may soon follow.

Early marriage is the next stage. The marriage ceremony marks the change from being single to being married. Although the marriage ceremony may seem less important than it was in the past, the change in way of life is still quite important. Marriages are much happier when the spouses realize that marriage calls for different ways of acting with families, friends and acquaintances and taking on the role of married persons graciously.

Marriage vows usually include the words "until death do us part" but in more and more marriages this means the death of caring for each other rather than death of the spouses. Marriage is not a commitment to be taken lightly. Becoming "as one flesh" suggests that two people begin to think as one. This is not easy to do in a world which stresses personal comfort and individual happiness.

Early marriage is also a time to come to terms with relatives. It sometimes takes a great deal of skill to keep on good terms with relatives while forming a separate family with new goals and ways of thinking which may differ greatly from those of the last generation. Spouses whose parents highly value education may find a great deal of opposition to their plans to open a restaurant rather than going to college.

Parents may offer to help a young couple financially. Although there may be clear expectations in return, this is usually not the case. However there may be subtle ways that parents let their wishes be known such as what they say when money is given. Although parents' expectations may well match the couple's wishes, it is best to know what these expectations are to avoid feuds.

Parents leave their mark long after their children themselves are married and on their own. It is surprising how many people fail to see that their attitudes about child rearing, husband and wife roles and family traditions are largely learned from their parents. Spouses often argue about how things should be done in one of these areas. They are stating their family beliefs rather than any right way of doing things. Although coming to terms with relatives is one of the most challenging tasks, there are others for the new family to consider. There are practical matters to face such as the need for two people to get ready in the morning rather than one, which cleaning and personal supplies to use, differing and maybe opposite eating and sleeping habits as well as differing amounts of sexual interest.

Friends can also be an issue. Each spouse has a group of friends and a certain way of entertaining and socializing. Making room for each other in their circle of friends or continuing individually with a different but agreed on schedule can be a challenge.

The wide variety among people almost always leads to differences of opinion and disagreements. Whether these lead to arguments depends on how well the spouses have learned to listen, bargain and satisfy each other. While there are many challenges in early marriage, meeting them successfully can lead to a very satisfying and rewarding relationship, necessary to manage problems which usually arise in later stages of marriage.

With the birth of children the marriage agreement becomes more fixed and more difficult to change. People who have second thoughts about marriage at this point may begin to feel trapped. If pregnancy was the reason for the marriage, the couple may not have had time to become a solid pair, which should usually happen in early marriage. Career goals and the wish to be good parents often conflict. In the past, this conflict has been stronger for women who up until recently stayed out of or left the job market to raise children. The beginning of school can also be a difficult time since it is then that the family's skill at raising children is put on public display.

Middle marriage is a time of family maturity. The parents become settled in their jobs and children generally need less attention. On the other hand it also is the time of mid-life crisis in which both spouses can see more clearly the rest of their lives with remaining limits and opportunities. Spouses also begin to realize that as the children leave, they will again be left with each other which reflects for better or worse the strength of the marriage and the closeness of the couple. It is at this time that people often choose to stay together or consider divorce. Children are also beginning to become adults and slowly but surely expect to be treated as adults by their parents.

In the stage of weaning parents from children, more challenges develop. Parents turn into grandparents, acting more or less like their own parents. The growing independence and leaving of children can be hard, especially if the children had to be helpers and friends for their parents. Parents must face the challenge of separating from children while staying involved with each other. As they think less about children, parents must look at what else they have in common besides children.

In retirement and old age, spouses must face the thought of being with each other twenty-four hours a day unless one or the other takes a retirement job. Although illness is more common at this stage, feeling sick can also be a way of keeping spouses connected with each other. This is also the stage where one or the other spouse must face being alone again if their partner dies first. Being taken care of may be necessary as many older people grow unable to meet all of their own needs. This stage of marriage poses many challenges. The creativity, flexibility and co-operation spouses bring to marriage at this stage leads directly to the degree of satisfaction they feel in their marriage.

HOW FAMILIES FAIL

Considering the many challenges facing families, it is not surprising that most families have difficulty at least once in a while. Fortunately, many families have the skill to settle their problems. Other families are not so lucky and become stuck with one or another challenge.

Stages of family development talked about above can be combined into pre-children, childbearing and post-children stages. One difficulty at the pre-children stage is failure to form a solid two-person relationship. Although married, spouses may keep fairly separate life-styles, allowing little involvement with each other. Some people may fail to separate from their families. It is very difficult to be a child in one family and a parent in another at the same time.

Also, people may marry for the wrong reason. A spouse may not know that he or she married to escape their own family. Later, when the escape has been made, there may be little reason to stay married. Sometimes this pattern continues until remarriage when spouses have to face another marriage without a good reason to continue.

During the child rearing stage, the obvious conflict is over how to raise children. Two parents may have been raised very differently and may either strongly agree or disagree with how the were raised. These strong opinions often clash with no good way to judge which way is best. Another common difficulty is what family therapists talk about as triangulation. Sometimes parents have failed to learn how to settle difficulties with each other, and form a bond with one of the children against their spouse.

The presence of a child offers parents an easy but hidden way to continue their fight with each other while allowing them to display less direct anger. An example is a man blaming his child for having too much of its mother's time when the real problem is that the parents do not know how to be close to each other. Another difficulty at this stage is the failure of a child to live up to what the parents expect. Parents many times look to their children to do what they were unable to do in their own lives. When the child also fails, parents sometimes think they have a bad child or that they have been poor parents.

In the post-children stage, there are other possible traps. Although usually more a risk for mothers, either parent may have made their chief goal in life the raising of successful children. This can be the focus of the family for many years. Even if this goal is accomplished, the children growing up and leaving can result in spouses feeling empty if they have not made an effort to find their own goals. At the other extreme, a risk usually greater for fathers, parents may become too involved in a career, leaving care of the children to others.

Spouses whose parents fought for years may have little idea of how parents can be close or how to solve differences. Then they carry their lack of skills in these areas into their own marriage so that the same pattern continues for another generation. People can also leave their families with poorly settled ideas of what a husband and father or wife and mother should be. One parent or the other may have been uncomfortable with or unsure of how to act as a spouse or parent. When children of such a marriage themselves marry, they may not know how to act as parents or spouses or may not know what to expect from a husband or wife.

Another pattern which some people learn from their parents is contradictory patterns of acting. For example, they may see their father as stern which he sees as appropriate for a real man. The sternness may also carry over into how he acts as a father, keeping him from showing understanding or caring which is very important for children to learn from both parents. The new spouse has learned from his father that being a man means being stern, but he may also wish to show warmth to his children. The example set by his father may leave him wondering how to be strict but also understanding.

Some people who grew up in families where parents argued a great deal learn to be peacemakers. In order to be able to live peacefully, they had to be the go-between in their parents' arguments. Some children learn how to listen to both parents and help them settle their differences.

More commonly, a child may learn to distract his or her parents by showing behavior or school problems or illness so that parents focus on them rather than arguing with each other. When such children themselves marry, they are poorly prepared for differences of opinion and may either avoid conflict or continue to change the subject by showing adult behavior problems such as drinking, acting helpless or developing mysterious illnesses.

Although ideas about sex roles have changed radically, people still come away from their families with some sense of what a man, and therefore a father and husband, should be and what a woman, and therefore a mother and wife, also should be. These ideas are often learned without being aware of them so that people sometimes do not realize their ideas about sex roles come from their parents.

There are some patterns which involve several generations and leave everyone feeling stuck. There may be a long-standing family tradition in which grandparents are highly involved in decisions about how to raise their grandchildren. In the most extreme case, four grandparents may all give opinions about childrearing, leaving parents wondering how to satisfy four grandparents while following their own ideas on parenting without offending any of the grandparents.

One mistake some families make is failing to see how complicated a family is. When they marry, there is just a two person relationship. When they have a child there are then four relationships. These consist of the original two person relationship between the parents, the relationship of each parent with the child, and the three person relationship of the whole family. Then consider the eleven relationships which result when a second child is born. The older the children, the more important it is to be aware of the network of relationships. There are a number of special problems which arise in families which will be considered separately.

HEALING FAMILIES

The stages of family development and the challenges they present can try the patience of any family. Families who can talk together well and who can find ways to work together may be able to weather the storms of family life without outside help. Other times, families are not able to find the problem but know that something is wrong. Families may also be able to identify a problem but may not know what to do about it.

In the past, mental health workers saw one person at a time, thought that problems took place inside an individual, were due to early childhood failures and could be solved by looking at the person's early life. A number of changes in this approach have taken place including looking at how people act and how they get along with each other without thinking too much about how things went in early life.

Then some mental health workers remembered that every person grows up in a family and that one person's problems could also be seen as difficulties in the family. Therapists who began to work with the whole family found that often problems could be solved more quickly than when working with one person. The whole family could become happier with the same time and effort that was previously spent with one individual. Consider what might happen to three people who seek out a family therapist in these fictitious examples.

Sarah noticed that she had trouble finishing things. She dropped out of college after three years. She was able to get a fairly good job in a large local business but left the job after five of the six months of probation. She had been close to marrying twice but both times backed out at the last minute. She had heard of family therapy and thought it might help.

She went to a family therapist even though her parents lived thousands of miles away and she had no relatives living close to her. Involving her family was not possible where she lived because they were not very well off financially and were also in poor health, making travel quite difficult for them.

The family therapist saw her anyway and spent time diagramming her family tree, looking at what part each person played in the family, how people got along and how they affected each other. Sarah and the therapist came to see that her parents sacrificed a great deal for their children. Twice her father passed up better jobs which would have involved moving. Her mother quit her job to be home with the children and used money she had been saving to start a business for her children's college education. Sarah realized that neither of her parents had gone beyond what their own parents had accomplished.

The therapist guessed that Sarah might be concerned that she would be betraying her parents and putting them down if she completed what she started and made a success of her life. During one session, the therapist had Sarah call her parents and talk with them about what they expected from her. She learned that her parents had mixed feelings about how they had lived their lives. Although they were glad they helped their children, they also felt they had missed several opportunities to make a better life for themselves and for the family. They certainly did not want to see Sarah limit herself or hold back from what she could be. This conversation and several more sessions talking with the therapist about what the conversation meant led Sarah to eventually finish college and find a fulfilling job. She decided to become settled in her job before she considered marriage.

Perry was a fifth grader who had done well in school until this year. But now he looked like he might fail and had also been suspended once for smoking in school and once for fighting. Neither of these had been problems before. His parents took Perry to a family therapist for help.

The therapist learned that Perry's father had a brief affair six months ago and that his parents had been separated for a short time. He also learned that Perry's grandmother was an alcoholic and never had much time for Perry's mother. Parry's mother in turn wanted to spend most of her time with Perry's father who had grown up in a family where the members were encouraged to take care of themselves.

Although at first Perry's father was flattered by how much time his wife wanted to spend with him, he later started to feel smothered and eventually found another woman with fewer demands. Although Perry's parents were back together, they still fought a lot. However they were doing less fighting lately since Perry had been getting into trouble. They now spent most of their time together worrying about him.

The therapist guessed that Perry was trying to distract his parents from their problems although he was not aware of doing this. The therapist got the family to talk about all of the things he had learned about the family. He helped the parents learn how to talk with each other without fighting. He helped Perry's mother realize that she had some special problems with closeness and dependence on others because of her mother's drinking and encouraged her to join an Adult Children of Alcoholics Group. He helped Perry's father learn how to share feelings and to realize that there were advantages to working with other people on personal problems rather than always trying to handle them alone. By the end of the school year, Perry was again doing well in school and had not been in any more trouble with the principal.

Bea had just finished high school and seemed very depressed to her parents. She had lost interest in her friends and activities and spent most of her time by herself. Her parents took her to a psychiatrist to see about medication but the psychiatrist referred them to their pastor who had been trained in family therapy. The pastor learned that Bea had been quite active and very involved with her friends until six months ago when her grandmother, who lived with the family for years, died suddenly.

Both of Bea's parents were highly involved in their jobs and were lucky to be able to take off two days for the funeral. Bea's mother had to take a trip out of town right after the funeral. The family immediately resumed their old pace and never really had time to talk about grandmother's death. The minister figured Bea was expressing the sadness about her grandmother's death for the whole family. The minister explained her idea to the family. She helped them plan a weekend in which they all made sure they had time to be together. On that weekend, they shared pictures, letters and stories about grandmother as well as all their good memories and sadness that she was no longer with them. Bea was soon able to be with her friends again and got on with her life. Although these cases may be overly simplified, they are the kinds of family situations which appear before family therapists. By learning to see what needs to be changed in the family, individuals and families can continue to grow or learn to grow in ways they could not before.

BLENDED FAMILIES

Years ago the great majority of stepfamilies resulted from death of parents. Now the great majority are as a result of divorce. Many children now find that they have more classmates with stepparents than with two original parents.

Many difficulties can result from divorce and remarriage. There can be a feeling of sadness that the original family is not still together. There can be worry about having enough money or about whether the new family will stay together. Young children especially keep hoping that their parents will get back together, sometimes long after they have married new spouses. Children often feel it is their fault their parents have divorced and carry a feeling of blame into the new family. Children sometimes show behavior problems such as truancy or shoplifting when the new family feels under pressure. It is also very common to see one parent as good and one as bad after a divorce, sometimes drawing the original parents into a contest to see who can be the better parent.

On the other hand, there are some advantages to blended families. There are usually more parents available than before to raise the children. Stepparents can see children with less emotion since they usually have not spent many years raising their children. Stepparents can also provide a network of relatives which may not otherwise be available.

Many blended families weather the storms of forming a new family. Others are not so lucky. Following are examples of what blended families might face and how they deal with their problems. Although these are not actual cases, they are similar to families who come for help.

Jerry divorced his wife after five years of marriage. He has two children who stayed with their mother. He came to realize that he liked to have time to himself and liked to be involved in sports all year round. His first wife had hoped to spend most of her time with him. Their arguments over how much time to spend together and what to do with the time finally led to their separation and divorce.

He later met and married Jan who was also divorced and had two school age children living with her who were about the same ages as Jerry's children. Jan left her husband because of his jealousy and need to control everything she did. He would not let her continue with her craft hobby and pressured her to quit her job.

Jerry and Jan thought they were perfect for each other. Jerry enjoyed continuing with his sports which Jan encouraged, and Jan found Jerry very supportive of her working and continuing with her crafts.

However Jerry's children had difficulty when they came to visit him because one or the other parent always seemed to be leaving to go to work or some adult activity. They were used to having both parents around and began to think that Jerry and his new wife did not want to be with them.

Jan's children were also confused by having a stepfather who was gone so much and also found their mother leaving them with a baby-sitter more often. Jan's husband and Jerry's wife both felt the children were being neglected and had even talked about child abuse charges for neglect. Jan and Jerry noticed all four children becoming quieter and showing little interest in anything. They had heard of blended families having difficulty but could not put their finger on any real problems. They decided to see a family therapist.

The therapist asked Jan and Jerry to come in with the four children. He noticed that Jan's children sat on one side of the room with her and Jerry's children sat on the other side with him. When he asked what they would like to change in the family, he heard Jan and Jerry say that they wanted everyone to be happy. He heard from all the children in various ways that they wanted to feel part of the family and get more attention. The therapist realized that both adults had gotten what they wanted by remarrying. But he also realized the children saw much less of their parents than they did before, even though there was less fighting.

The therapist suggested a number of changes after he got to know the family. He suggested activities such as scouts and neighborhood sports programs for the children which took place during times the parents were out. He also suggested that the parents find ways to share what they were good at with the children, such as coaching for Jerry and craft demonstrations for children for Jan. Eventually the children realized that even though their parents were not around as much they still cared. They also welcomed their parents' participation in their activities.

Scott was a fourteen year old boy who had lived with his mother Ann since his father left when he was four. He had little contact with his father who had only seen him once since he was twelve. He had learned to do many repairs around the house and was quite valuable to his mother who did not earn very much at her job and could not pay someone for repairs.

Ann met a mechanic, Charlie. In addition to their enjoying each other's company and sharing common goals, she felt Charlie would be good for Scott since they shared a common interest in mechanical pursuits. Indeed, they seemed to get along well at first. However, six months after they married, Scott started coming home very late and several times had been drinking. Also, he seemed to have lost his interest in mechanics and found other things to do when Charlie had projects planned for the two of them.

They also found their way to a family therapist when Scott was suspended from school for showing up drunk. In the first session, Ann and Charlie sat on one side of the room and Scott sat on the other side. Ann and Charlie said they both wanted Scott to be part of the new family and tried hard to include him in all of their activities. Scott had no explanation for his drinking or his tendency to avoid being home. He also had no idea what he wanted to change in the family.

The therapist asked Scott to place himself in the room to show how he saw the family and to place his parents where he saw them as being in the family. Scott placed his parents facing each other and holding hands. He placed himself in the corner facing the wall. The therapist realized that she was seeing Scott's feeling of having lost his place of importance in the family to Charlie.

The therapist suggested that Scott and Charlie find three half hours per week to spend together. During this time, Scott was to pretend to teach Charlie how to do electrical repairs at which Scott was quite good. Although all three family members thought it rather silly, they tried it. After several weeks of "teaching," Scott and Charlie found they enjoyed being with each other and began to make plans for the weekend that did not involve mechanics. The drinking also stopped.

Although not all blended family problems are this simple or easy to fix, these are some of the kinds of problems blended families face. It is also easier for an outsider such as a family therapist to see what the problem is and to suggest a solution than it is to see problems and solutions from within.

FAMILIES WITH SPECIAL PROBLEMS

A number of special problems arise in some families which can destroy the family if not handled properly. The following are not the only serious problems families face but are examples of such problems.

Alcoholism in the family is more noticed and talked about than in the past. A school may notice a child coming in dirty and hungry on a regular basis. The father is known to have a good job and the family lives in a good neighborhood. A visit to the home by a school social worker at 10:00 AM finds the mother intoxicated.

Such situations can happen for a number of reasons. The mother as well as her husband may have come from families where alcoholism was present but ignored. Families of alcoholics often cover for them and secretly hope the problem will go away. Solving this problem means first admitting it exists. The alcoholic may need inpatient treatment or AA. The family may need the support of Alanon or family therapy to change into a family that supports sobriety rather than alcoholism.

In another family, a thirteen year old girl may refuse to attend gym class and is most definite about not changing in the locker room. This pattern might reflect her shame about her developing body due to incest with her stepfather which has gone on for over a year.

Changing this pattern usually means starting with legal charges in family and criminal court. This is usually necessary to force the offending parent into taking the problem seriously and following through with treatment. Sometimes a jail sentence is also necessary to get his attention. Once the offender is ready to go to work on the problem, individual or group treatment is helpful to get impulses under control and to learn better ways to meet sexual needs. The child may need some help with her own feelings about being abused and about what happens to the family when she tells about the incest. The mother usually needs help with her feelings of guilt and anger. The family can then be rebuilt by reconnecting mother and child, improving the marriage and family, helping the family as a whole to find new ways to live together.

Physical disability can also be a major hurdle. A child who seemed normal in every way may later be found not to respond to the parents. It may be discovered that the child is deaf. One of the first reactions is denial. Families do not want to face the possibility of their child being abnormal. The hope for a cure stays for a while and may prompt many visits to doctors.

When it is clear that their child will remain deaf, parents are faced with how to raise a child with whom they cannot communicate. In the past, some deaf children were not allowed to learn sign language so that they would be forced to try to make their way in a hearing world. Now more parents realize that the deaf do not just have a different language but also have their own culture and way of life. Parents now are more willing to learn sign language themselves so that they can share more of their children's lives.

Learning disabilities are very confusing for most children, parents and often for schools as well. A child may seem retarded, lazy or a behavior problem. Children are often treated for years as though they have one of these three problems. Psychological testing can show that such a child is of average or above average intelligence, but might not be able to deal with letters or words through hearing or seeing them. Children sometimes would rather look lazy or be seen as clowns rather than admit they cannot read.

By the time a learning disability is discovered, there is often a long history of seeing the child in some other, usually negative, way. A classroom setting in which the child can learn to use the abilities he or she has, is obviously most important. Individual work with the child or family counseling may also be helpful for the child and family to recognize what the child is good at and to help develop his or her strengths.

A child who sets fires can be annoying at best. At worst is the risk of burning down the house or people dying. This is a symptom which most families take very seriously. This dramatic behavior seldom fails to get the family's attention.

Fire setting can be a child's way of showing anger, fear of being left alone or a way of expressing the family's confusion when no one else in the family seems to know what to do. Setting a fire can be a very effective, but dangerous, way to get the family into treatment. Helping the family to pay attention to the fire setting child, and to look at problems they couldn't face before usually stops the fire setting as well as helping the family to improve its life.

A child or teenager who runs away from home is saying that he or she feels safer or more in control on the streets than at home. There can be many reasons for running away. One of the most common is feeling misunderstood. For example, parents may not want to restrict their children and may allow them to do most anything they want to. When their children become teenagers, the parents decide it is time to set some limits. If they have seldom set any limits before, it will be difficult for teenagers to suddenly accept limits from parents who did not seem to care what they did before. Children who have not learned to accept limits or at least compromise with their parents will have trouble taking anything but an extreme stand such as threatening to run away.

There are many other situations which pressure families. Many of these are best handled with the help of a family therapist. As mentioned before, family therapy is only one approach to problems which take place in the family. However it is often the quickest and most direct way to manage the problem. Mental health professionals are sometimes trained to work with families as are some clergy. While seeking help from an outsider can be stressful, it can teach the skills a family can use to manage other crises which might arise in the future.

THE CRAZY TEEN YEARS

Many parents feel that as their teenage children approach age sixteen, they turn into creatures other than human. Sometimes they appear to speak a different language, possess alien values and seem to have lost all sense of what their parents have wanted for them since they were born.

Some parents blame themselves for this turn of events and scratch their heads while thinking back and looking for one thing they did to send their child off in this strange direction. Others may feel their child has had "an encounter of the third kind" which included a brain transplant. In any case, it may appear that communication has abruptly ceased and that little can be done to restore it. Since parents are feeling so isolated from their children at this point, they seldom realize that their children have been entertaining similar thoughts about them. Even the "what have I done wrong" feeling is not uncommon among adolescents, especially when there are serious marital or family problems.

Some parents and/or teens turn to a counselor or therapist to help them sort out the tangle of misunderstandings and hard feelings. Others seek foster placement or other public intervention. Mutual isolation and making the best of a bad situation is another alternative. Despite the course of action taken, emotions run high on both sides and there is often very little logical examination of the events and issues involved. Emotions prevail.

It is often difficult to know whether such problems are a normal part of family development or whether something is terribly wrong. It is this confusion which further muddles any attempt to sort things out. There are several levels on which the problems can be viewed.

First is the "normal development" view. As teens grow older, they come nearer to total independence. The time when they must assume complete responsibility for their actions gets closer. A person who must take a driver's test does not remain in the back seat until the day of the test. A teen who must decide for himself or herself cannot be expected to follow orders until the day he or she leaves the home and then make responsible decisions.

Like many other skills, being independent takes time to learn and requires some practice. Being an adult and being responsible are skills that should begin as early in life as possible. There are many things a child can safely decide alone. Which clothes to wear or what cereal to have for breakfast can be decided at an early age without earth shaking consequences. Children who have been allowed to make increasingly more important decisions as they grow older are in a much better position to assume responsibility as adults than children who have had everything decided for them. This does not mean that children always understand the consequences of their decisions or even what choices they have. This is where parent-child communication plays such an important part.

Children are naturally inquisitive if their curiosity is not stifled by their parents or school. They are always wondering "what happens if...?" Taking the time to explain alternatives and their consequences may seem like a lot of work. However, if such a pattern of communication can be established early in life, children are much more likely to discuss major issues with their parents when the time comes. What if a child makes a bad decision? It does hurt to make a mistake and have to live with it. But this is part of learning to be responsible. A child who is protected from the consequences of all bad decisions has great difficulty learning the importance of deciding carefully when the time comes.

Beyond the level of normal development are extraordinary circumstances which complicate the maturing process. Death of a parent, separation or divorce of parents, compicate an already difficult task. The remaining parent often must focus on his or her own emotional survival while attention is shifted from the child. It is easier in a time of crisis to tell children what to do than it is to take the extra time to explain things. However, if the parent is in crisis, the child usually is too, often feeling at least partially responsible for the crisis. It is particularly important to take time to help a child deal with his or her own role in the crisis.

Further difficulties result from emotional problems suffered by anyone in the family. This is a rather involved issue bearing separate consideration. However, it should be obvious that a relationship which is so often hampered by ordinary events can be seriously affected by the added stress of emotional difficulties.

There are several implications of all this for minimizing conflict between parents and teens. First, do not wait until teens are older. The sooner parents can begin helping their children make decisions for themselves, the easier it will be for teens to make the transition to independence when the time comes.

Second, parents moving from the "boss" role to that of helpful consultant whenever possible encourages children to take healthy risks after seeking parental advice. Children then realize that what happens to them is largely a result of their own actions. Children and teens, busy learning the consequences of their own behavior, are much more likely to be able to improve their behavior the next time around than are those who have everything decided for them.

Third, many parents who were neglected or deprived of their own parents' attention, go overboard in caring for their own children and can keep them from developing healthy decision making skills while trying to be helpful.

Finally, despite all that is written about parenting, there has not yet emerged a foolproof way of raising children. Parents who are honest realize that raising children is as much a growth process for themselves as for their children. A healthy respect for parents' own limitations is the best way to help children learn to respect their parents' strengths. It is always helpful to remember that raising children is not just a task, but a living relationship calling for cooperative growth on the part of parent and child.

CHAPTER 6

SPIRITUALITY

Day to day life can be difficult to make sense of without a larger context. Our sense of spirituality is a way of making sense of our lives. The idea of spirituality can be daunting for some people. This chapter is an approach to explaining spirituality in a simple and practical way.

MENTAL HEALTH AND SPIRITUALITY

Some religions have been cautious about mental health counseling, thinking that counselors may undermine spiritual values. Some therapists have been skeptical of religion, thinking that religions may oversimplify psychological issues and fear that spiritual thinking may overlook or even worsen serious mental and emotional conditions.

Are mental health and spiritual approaches to life mutually exclusive, or can they overlap or even complement each other? Part of the answer lies in how each approach is looked at. Neither is complete in itself.

Psychology is based on what we experience through our five senses and on how we act on what our senses tell us. Mental health efforts are intended to understand, predict and change human behavior. Psychological approaches do not usually focus on the larger meaning of why we act the way we do. Therapists ask what, when, where and how questions, but usually see "why" questions as not very useful.

Spirituality is based on understanding the reasons for our existence. Spirituality considers what we are doing on earth, what our actions mean in our lives and what they mean to others, as well as the larger meaning of our lives beyond our own experience.

No one religion has the corner on spirituality and it is quite possible to have a spiritual focus without belonging to any organized religion. There are many paths to spirituality and various religions can be seen as different kinds of road maps to help find the way.

Psychology looks at what influences our behavior and what brings us to act in certain ways. Psychological counseling helps people to change or look in different ways at those influences so that we can live less troublesome lives. Mental health approaches ignore thoughts about why we are on earth or trying to understand what the point of our lives actually is.

Spirituality is an approach to understanding why we are here on earth. It ties us to our Creator or Higher Power in the sense of looking for an understanding of a master plan for humanity and how our lives fit into this plan. While our understanding is limited by our humanity, we have an awareness of there being a level of reality beyond ourselves. We cannot look objectively at the whole of reality since we are part of what we are trying to understand.

While spirituality focuses on understanding why we are here, it does not address the mechanics of how we act and how to change our behavior.

Briefly summarized, mental health is about how we behave and how our behavior can change, while spirituality is about why we bother to act at all. Mental health looks at psychologically healthy ways to live while spirituality seeks ways of making our actions more meaningful in a larger context. Looked at in this way, mental health and spirituality complement each other and can give a fairly complete understanding of ourselves.

Gary Zukav, in *Seat of the Soul*, defines spiritual psychology as "a disciplined and systematic study of what is necessary to the health of the soul." The problem is that there is no universal agreement on what the soul is.

In psychology, the soul has been referred to as a "ghost in the machine" or something mysterious which is beyond the scope of psychological thinking. Christian thinking holds that the soul continues to exist after death and that the body is the way the soul deals with the material world. Jewish beliefs are less definite about the fate of the individual soul, but expect that God will reward those who live good lives in the afterlife. Oriental religious thinking sees the individual "soul" as something to be diminished as we merge with the larger reality. Of course, some people think that there is no such thing as a soul and that our existence begins and ends with our conception and death.

Theories about how to live our lives and what our lives mean are in no short supply. But, in practice, what does all this mean in our everyday lives? Is there a way to live in an emotionally healthy way and also keep a spiritual focus?

A good first step is to take some time away from our usual busy routine. When we are busy, we are often on automatic pilot and follow our usual path without thinking much about what puts us on this path or where we are headed.

Time out could take place in a church. It could also be in a cave, forest, garden or on a beach. If you spend your daily life in one of these places, you may need to find somewhere even more exotic to do your thinking.

Meditation or clearing our minds is a useful way to disconnect from everyday concerns. This is something like putting our car in neutral and looking to see what is around us rather than driving frantically from one place to another. It is amazing how many wonderful experiences we miss in our rush to get everything done.

Once we are able to back off from our everyday whirlwind, here are some questions we may ask ourselves to see if we are in balance.

If we act in a certain way, will this lead to a greater sense of peace with ourselves and the rest of the world? Will acting in a certain way contribute anything useful to our sense of well being or to the well being of the rest of the world? Can we enjoy doing what we are doing without hurting anyone else?

Living healthy lives, psychologically and spiritually, is a

process and one which we can work on day by day. We can work toward balancing and making sense of our lives along a number of dimensions. We often go along in our lives without considering whether we know where we are headed.

Getting balanced psychologically and spiritually is not easy. Some of us can do it on our own. But most of us need some help from others. Friends can be helpful if they are further along the path toward spiritual or psychological health than we are. Spiritual advisers and mental health counselors can be helpful if they are tuned in to spiritual and psychologically healthy ways of living. Don't be afraid to ask.

SPIRITUALITY FOR THE COMMON PERSON- AWAKENING

The word spirituality makes some people squeamish. Visions may arise of monks huddled around an altar, chanting in Latin. What relevance does this have for us in our everyday life? I have often wondered what spirituality really meant. A chemical dependency counselor I knew, affectionately known as Popsie, once described spirituality as "the awakening to the goodness and joy for which you were created." His definition seemed simple enough and I didn't give it much thought at first. It has come back to my mind many times in the past few years and lately I have been thinking about it even more.

Awakening is the first part of the definition and I would like to consider it with you first. We awaken from sleep in different ways. Sometimes we are startled awake. Sometimes we feel like we are still dreaming and sometimes we are immediately wide awake. Regardless of how we do it, awakening means coming into a different state of awareness or consciousness.

In addition to coming out of sleep, awakening can mean coming to see things in a new light. It can be a realization that there are more dimensions to life than we thought. We can awaken to new possibilities in our lives or we can choose not to.

Having a closed mind shuts off our connection with the universe. Seeing only what is within our limited experience keeps us narrow minded and limits our potential for growth as a person. There are many possibilities for our life we will never see if we do not awaken to them. Einstein defined craziness as "endlessly repeating the same process, hoping for a different result." In his book *In Search of Excellence*, Tom Peters said the same thing in a little different way, "If you always do what you always did, you always get what you always got." I can remember doing the same thing over and over, getting frustrated each time. I finally let some new ideas into my mind and found there was an easier and more satisfying way of doing things. New ideas come from reading, sharing our experiences with others, watching how others do things or listening to someone wiser than us. We might also allow new ideas in just by being quiet within ourselves and letting them come to us in the silence.

Awakening means being flexible, open to new possibilities in our lives, and looking outside ourselves to find the larger meaning of our lives. Looking at a gear by itself does not show us its meaning. Seeing it as part of a machine shows it in a new light. Our lives have a larger meaning when we look at them in the context of our family, neighborhood, global community and the universe.

Awakening is learning to see our lives from a larger perspective, for what our lives mean to others and for how we can work with others toward a better human community. The specifics of this will be explored next.

SPIRITUALITY FOR THE COMMON PERSON-GOODNESS

Sometimes we think of goodness as trite as when someone exclaims, "Oh, my goodness!" We may think of it as sickening sweetness as in Goody Two Shoes or Pollyanna. Goodness is such a common word it is hard to find a deeper meaning in it. What is goodness? I wondered what the dictionary had to say about it and did not learn much except that the word comes from Middle English and means the state of being good.

One way of looking at goodness is the potential to go beyond the limited world of our own experience. We have gifts unique to ourselves which may benefit one other person or maybe many people. Anything from a smile to finding a vaccine for a major illness makes at least some difference in the world.

Martha Graham, the famous dancer and choreographer, put it this way, "There is a vitality, like a life force that is translated through you into actions. And because there is only one of you in all time, this expression is unique, and if you block it, it will never exist through any other medium and be lost." She saw the unique contribution each of us has to make to the world. Civilization will still go on and history will continue if we choose not to use our gifts, but there will be something missing without our contribution.

We all have the potential for goodness as well as for evil, and a third alternative of not acting at all. Some of us had the good fortune to be treated by our parents as special and were frequently reminded of how amazing we were. Parents in some families rejoice at our accomplishments. With this level of support, it is easier to risk trying to reach our potential. Without that support, it may be difficult to see ourselves as being of very much value to the world. We might decide to get revenge on others for our lot in life or decide that we have nothing to offer to others and not try.

The twelfth century visionary, Hildegard of Bingen, wrote, "God has arranged everything in the universe in consideration of everything else... Everything that is in the heavens, on the earth, and under the earth, is penetrated with connectedness, penetrated with relatedness."

Elizabeth Lesser, in *The New American Spirituality*, goes on to say that, "Our task as human souls is to live as individual beings in connection with others and all things. We can be unique without being better than anyone else, without being special."

While we all have a unique contribution to make to the world, we are still part of a grand plan set in motion by God. We have the ability to choose whether to contribute what we have to the grand plan or let it go on without us. What do you plan to do with your gifts?

SPIRITUALITY FOR THE COMMON PERSON- JOY

Joy is another one of those words which means everything and nothing. The dictionary defines it as, "a state or a feeling of great pleasure, happiness, or delight." Most of us know what joy feels like. Joy is a feeling we have when we open just the right Christmas or birthday present. It is also what we feel when we find and accept in our lives the special gifts God has given us. These are the abilities and traits which make us unique, a little different from everyone else. Joy is also the feeling we get when we use these gifts to best advantage, enhancing our own or someone else's life.

I once saw a tee shirt that read, "Life's a bitch, and then you die." This is the opposite of joy. There are times when life seems difficult and when we have to face things we would rather not face. Eastern religions have a concept of Karma which some people have taken to mean predestination, meaning we have a lot in life we are destined to accept. Another way of looking at Karma is that choices we make determine what happens in our lives. We do tend to get what we focus on. Those who think about how awful their lives are, tend to have awful lives. But people who look for the positive tend to be much more joyful, even if they are facing great adversity.

Steve DeNunzio, a wise friend of mine, talks about accepting problems in our lives as a signal from God that there is something we need to attend to. The motivational speaker Napoleon Hill, stated that "inside every adversity is contained the seed of an at least equal benefit." Once we find the benefit hidden in our adversity, we can be joyful about the outcome of situations which do not seem very promising at first.

Sometimes our goodness comes out when things seem at their worst. It is almost as if the gold of the joy inside us needs to be smelted in the fire of our troubles.

Rather than facing life's difficulties, some of us tend to sedate ourselves with alcohol, drugs, food or other addictive behaviors. Our addictions so consume us that we no longer have the energy to find our strengths and rejoice in them. For those of us who have been down this path, the joy comes in having the courage to eventually face life without our addictions, learn to overcome them and find out what we are really capable of.

Sometimes it takes a great deal of courage to break out of our chains. When we finally do, we can begin to feel like birds who soar freely in the air enjoying the journey and adventure of where the winds of life take us.

SPIRITUALITY FOR THE COMMON PERSON- FOR WHICH YOU WERE CREATED

There has been a recent renewal of controversy in the news about teaching creation or evolution. People are entrenched on both sides taking extreme positions, pitting science against faith.

It seems to me that science and faith are not mutually exclusive. If you look at a fish, a pig and a human at one stage of embryonic development, they are indistinguishable. This could be taken as evidence that one developed from another or that they all had the same creator. Why could not both be true so that different creatures were created to develop from one another over the ages?

Trying to make sense of God or creation with our limited understanding is like "trying to bicycle across an ocean" to quote Elizabeth Lesser in *The New American Spirituality*. We have a great deal of trouble understanding our place in creation. How much harder is it to understand God with the few clues we have to go by?

Some people seem to feel that if we can't make sense of God, there is no use thinking about a Creator. George Bernard Shaw said that if when he died, it turned out there was a God, they would sit down and talk about it man to man. Other people spend their lives trying to make sense of God from a scientific or theological point of view or give themselves over to marveling about what we have learned about the universe.

It is not really possible to prove God exists. There are so called natural proofs of the existence of God, but they make much more sense once the existence of God is accepted on faith. One "proof" is order in the universe. It is extremely unlikely that everything that has happened since the universe started took place by chance. Order and balance in the universe are quite difficult to explain without thinking of how everything got started and what keeps it going. Even the Big Bang theory of the beginning of the universe leaves unanswered the question of why there was a big bang to get things started in the first place.

In the end, it seems we have to take our creation, as well as God, on faith which is as it should be. Our being created is what ties together the awakening, goodness and joy which we have just addressed. It gives us a meaning beyond ourselves and a purpose for existing, as well as a way to make sense of our lives.

Hildegard of Bingen put it as, "All living creatures are, so to speak, sparks from the radiation of God's brilliance, and these sparks emerge from God like the rays of the sun. There is no creature without some kind of radiance."

It seems that, by our nature, we are radiant if we let ourselves be, opening like a flower and sharing our beauty with each other.

FINDING OUR GIFTS

Do you remember your last birthday? What gifts did you receive? Some may stand out, others you may have forgotten. Most people like to receive gifts, or at least did in childhood. What if you had gifts which stayed with you throughout your life? You do, you know.

Each of us has unique gifts left us by God to find along our path in life. Some people seem to have a great many gifts, and some appear to have only a few. What are your special gifts? Maybe you are a good listener. Maybe you can easily make people laugh. Maybe you are a good problem-solver. Maybe you can stay calm no matter how difficult a situation gets.

How do you know what your gifts are? If you pay attention, people will tell you. Relatives may tell you they always know they can count on you to understand how they feel. Friends may call you when they need to get a job done. Children may want to be near you when you visit.

The first step is to be aware of your gifts. Did you ever stop to think about what you are good at or what comes easily to you? You may not think of your gifts as anything special. My son once told me that metal sculpture was easy and that anyone could do it. However, I don't know anyone else whose first piece received a gold medal in a national competition.

Once you recognize your gifts, the next step is to start using them. Does it do anyone any good if you are a good problem solver but you keep your opinion to yourself while others scratch their heads? Your special gifts are meant to be shared with others and to make your life meaningful.

The third step is to recognize others' gifts. There are people we may find annoying or very much unlike ourselves, inclining us to avoid them. Even these people have special gifts, although it may be a little more work to find them.

I remember a receptionist who had trouble remembering callers' names or what they wanted and often lost messages altogether. Once, when the whole staff was at a meeting, a very depressed woman came in early for her appointment. When the staff got back from the meeting, they found the receptionist doing a very good job of comforting the woman.

We generally like it when others notice and appreciate our gifts. We will probably find that others are more likely to share their gifts if we notice and appreciate them too.

CHAPTER 7

HOLIDAYS

We take time on holidays to think back on our relationships and the progress of our lives. Following are some reflections for when you area ready to take time out and consider where you are with your life.

EVERY DAY IS TIME TO START AGAIN

There is a Latin hymn, "Hodie Christus Natus Est- Today Christ is Born." A friend of mine who thinks deeply about such things wondered how Christ could be born today when his birth and all the events that followed it took place two centuries ago. I hadn't really considered the implications or wondered just what we were saying in the hymn. It is a good question though.

The historical Jesus lived many centuries ago and is not born again in the flesh each Christmas. Likewise, we are born in our bodies only once. Christians value the symbolic rebirth in baptism to a new way of life. Some religious traditions stress being born again as an adult, inviting people to a mature commitment to a personal relationship with Jesus. Hindus believe in reincarnation as a way of working toward a more complete purification of the soul.

The new year is seen as a time of renewal, giving us a chance to start again with resolutions to improve various aspects of our lives. We also see spring as a rebirth of nature, largely dormant through the winter.

Sometimes we get stuck in a rut, living in ways we know are not healthy for us physically, emotionally or spiritually. We tend to put off making changes until the arrival of one of the major events mentioned above. We think to ourselves, "I should change this about myself" or "I will have to think about this." It can be some time before we actually make any changes or even give them serious consideration.

No matter how badly we have botched up our lives today, or how long we have lived in a way we regret, today ends when we go to sleep tonight. We can leave whatever we need to in the day just passed and start a new chapter in our lives tomorrow. We don't have to wait for a major event in our lives to make a change.

We can start doing or stop doing some things in our lives just by deciding to do so. Starting a new way of life may not be easy, since it takes concentration and practice to break old habits.

There may be other things in our lives we know we need to change, but we might not know how to go about making the changes. We can gather information from reading, seek advice from someone we think could help, or pursue professional counseling if need be. We can start on these changes today.

We have the choice each day to continue living the way we did yesterday or to start living in a way which is better for us, as well as for those we care about and those we meet in the course of our everyday lives. We can wake up and continue business as usual. Or we can look in the mirror, wish ourselves a happy new day, and proceed to make our life a little better.

MAKING RESOLUTIONS WORK

Do you remember any of your New Year's resolutions from last year? If so, how did you do? Most of us who do make resolutions are serious about keeping them, but somehow our resolve comes undone soon after the new year gets underway.

Making a resolution is a step toward making some real changes. We usually start with a daydream or idea. We may move to a resolution. The final step is action. The road between intent and accomplishment seems long and dark and is often littered with resolutions which don't quite make it for one reason or another. We would be in better shape if we ate more sensibly or got more exercise. We would feel more accomplished if we learned the skill we promised ourselves we would. Feeling more prosperous would follow being more careful with our money.

What happened to all these fine resolutions? Perhaps we acted impulsively, not considering whether we had the ability to follow through with them. Were they all that important to us in the long run?

Rather than latching onto the first resolution which comes to mind, we could stop to think before resolving. What have we learned about ourselves over the last year? Did we find or develop any new skills? Did we discover any strengths or weaknesses in how we go about things? Did we learn there were things we can't do?

With these thoughts in mind, it should be easier to decide on a resolution which moves us along the road toward our life goals and uses strengths and skills we know we have.

Once we have a resolution, the next step is to keep it in mind as the year progresses. One possibility would be to write a few key words on our calendars on the first of each month, reminding us to stop and think about how we did with our resolution in the past month. It is also a chance to think about how we can refine our resolution over the next month. If a month is too long, try doing it once a week. We might discover as we go along that we bit off a little too much and our resolution is somewhat too ambitious. Maybe there is part of the resolution we can work on this year and save the rest for next year. Maybe we will discover we don't quite have the skills to carry off our resolution. A mini-goal could be to learn the necessary skills from someone more proficient than we are and then return to our resolution.

Keeping track of our resolutions, progress and accomplishments will help us stay more focused on our long term goals, using our skills and strengths. We will become more aware of what we have to offer and learn to appreciate ourselves. Maybe next December we will be able to look back over the past year and see we have become a little more of the person we would like to be.

THANKSGIVING

Thanksgiving is the start of the holiday season which lasts until we recover from New Year's Day. It is a busy time of gathering with friends and relatives we may not have seen for some time.

For most people it is a time when social life goes into high gear. We get so busy that we have little time to stop and think about what Thanksgiving means. In our country, the tradition started with our remembrance of Native Americans, then called Indians, keeping our early settlers from starving to death during the harsh colonial winters. Considering the history of Native American people in our country, it did not take us long to forget how grateful we were.

Thanksgiving seems to have become a time to be grateful for what we have received from God or from each other. We tend to focus on the past. We take time out for a little while to be grateful for former favors and then forget the whole thing until next year.

What else could we do? Consider an example. Your best friend is concerned about something that is troubling you. He goes to great lengths to find a book for you about your difficulty and gives you the book. You sincerely appreci-ate your friend's efforts and his wisdom in recognizing your problem. You tell your friend how grateful you are and really mean it. Then you put the book on a shelf and never open it. You have wasted an opportunity to benefit from the gift.

When we stop to consider what we are grateful for at Thanksgiving, we usually think of our financial well being, our health or the people who love us. We can go beyond this. We can concentrate on gathering more money just for the sake of having it in the bank or we can learn to be stewards of our money for the betterment of our own and others' lives. We can just enjoy being healthy at the moment or we can take our good health as a challenge to do what we can to stay healthy. We can be happy we have loving people around us and stop there or we can find ways to return their caring and enhance their lives as well as our own.

We tend to be thankful for things which have already happened and hope to change the things we don't like in our lives. We could also give thanks that our lives are set on a course which will bring us all the good things we need, even though they have not arrived yet.

Perhaps it is hardest to be grateful for the adversities in our lives. Rather than complaining about our misfortunes, what if we look at them as lessons we can use to improve our lives? This is not an easy thing to do, but in the end it leads us in a positive direction rather than keeping us focused on our troubles. What is your choice?

CHRISTMAS

What usually comes to mind as Christmas nears? Before we have a chance to think about it, we are bombarded by ads to buy everything under the sun. We have to wade through all the commercial trappings to get to the spiritual aspects of Christmas.

Christmas is about a birthday, that of Jesus. To some people, Jesus is the Son of God, part of the Trinity which constitutes God. To others, he was a good man who brought some new ideas about how to live peacefully with each other. To still others, Jesus seems irrelevant to their daily lives.

Regardless of our beliefs, I think we can all agree that a baby named Jesus was born about 2000 years ago. Although not an infrequent occurrence, the birth of any baby is truly a miracle. The study of embryology shows us the thousands of steps which must take place successfully in order for a fertilized egg to become a living, breathing baby.

If you know someone who has a baby and you visit the baby on two occasions a week apart, you will be amazed at the changes that have taken place between your two visits. The baby, who once stared unresponsively, learns to smile, roll over, wave, clap hands, stand and eventually communicate with you.

Holding a newborn baby brings us a sense of awe and a reverence for life rather than allowing us to take life for granted. It is a reminder of how far we have come since emerging from the womb. A baby's innocence reminds us that we can look at things around us in a fresh way, no matter how jaded we have become over the years.

Babies hold great promise for the world. Alexander the Great, Churchill, Michelangelo, Mozart and Shakespeare all started out as babies. Who could tell, looking at any of them as babies, what their lives would hold? What do you think your parents imagined for you when you were born? If you have children, what did you imagine for them?

Sometimes we think we only have one chance in life. We feel trapped by how our parents raised us, how we have allowed ourselves to become mired down or how others have treated us. We sometimes dwell on our physical or mental limitations or those imposed by bad health. Somehow it seems easier to think about what we can't do than what we can do. I remember the story of a woman who had no arms but became an excellent office manager and private secretary using her toes. Sometimes it is our very limitations which point us toward our capabilities.

So what does all this have to do with Christmas? We have a chance to be reborn with Jesus, not just on Christmas but every day. What if we woke up tomorrow morning with none of the old thinking which keeps us from trying something new? What might we be able to do if we did not let our negative thinking hold us back? Would you like to try it?

DID SOMEONE STEAL CHRISTMAS?

There is a growing concern that Christmas has been stolen. Columns and letters to the editor decry the commercialization of the season. I have been asked by more than one person to **please** write about what has happened to Christmas.

Christmas decorations start appearing in stores around Halloween and the pace of advertising for Christmas buying starts to gather steam steadily as the fall progresses. Business commentaries gauge the pace of Christmas buying and the effect on the national economy. Many stores count on the Christmas season for a large percent of their income. Although we have come to see stores as large conglomerates, there are still many stores run by families who count on holiday sales for a large part of their survival. Christians invariably rue the commercial focus of a cherished season. Maybe it is more pronounced this year since the economy has been weak for so long and is finally rebounding.

Christians talk as if Christmas was theirs first, and then usurped by commercial interests. Do you know why Christmas is celebrated in late December? Prior to Christianity, late December was devoted to the Roman feast of Saturnalia, a pagan celebration of the deity, Saturn. Early Christians decided to celebrate the birth of Christ in late December as a way of substituting a spiritual focus for a pagan one. In that sense, Christians stole the holiday season from the pagans.

Although Christmas has taken on a strong commercial tone in our culture, we as citizens are not required to adopt this focus. That is the benefit of living in a democracy. We can choose to adopt or ignore what we want as long as what we do is legal. Judging by European and Middle Eastern history, living in a country with a state religion had its dangers and drawbacks as well.

Regardless of what goes on around us, we are free to take whatever focus we choose. We do not have to buy gifts until there is no room left on our credit cards. Santa Claus and Xmas wreaths do not have to be our only symbols of Christmas. Alvin and the Chipmunks do not have to constitute our holiday music.

We can keep Jesus and the spiritual meaning of Christmas in our hearts. We can teach our children quiet reverence for the events in the manger rather than the boisterous bustle of Christmas shopping. We can give our time, creativity and caring to those we love rather than, or in addition to, buying presents.

Regardless of what goes on in the culture around us, we do not have to be "of the world," even though we do have to live in it, unless we are hermits. Even though it appears more obvious at this time of year, there are always distractions from the purpose we set for our lives. Rather than complaining about them, it is better to put our efforts into maintaining our spiritual focus.

Hodie, Christus natus est (Today, Christ is born.)

CHAPTER 8

ADDICTIONS

Many of us have patterns of behavior difficult to change. We may also have friends or relatives struggling with their own addictions. This chapter suggests some ways of approaching addictions complicating our own lives as well as those of people we care about.

RECOGNIZING OUR ADDICTIONS

Addiction has been defined in various ways. Chemical addictions have been defined as "a compulsive need for and use of habit forming drugs" or "A progressive, chronic, primary, relapsing disorder that involves features such as a compulsion to use a chemical, loss of control over the use of a substance and continued use of a drug in spite of adverse consequences of its use." Both definitions suggest a pattern of compulsive behavior which complicates our lives and makes them feel less worth living. They also make us harder to be near. Regardless of how we define addictions, they are behaviors which cause trouble for ourselves and those around us. There is some research evidence that chemical addictions may be genetically based. It is possible that we inherit other such patterns as well.

Addictions can be physical, psychological or both. Physical ones, such as heroin, have biological effects on the body and are marked by withdrawal symptoms when we stop using the chemical involved. Psychological dependency is coming to depend on the feeling we get from consistently turning to our troublesome behavior pattern.

Addictions can develop in different ways. Sometimes we might experiment with a drug to see what it is like and find ourselves having trouble living without it. We might start using a drug to manage pain and get so used to the euphoric feeling that we continue using pain killers long after they are needed. We can also develop psychological dependence on compulsive sexual behavior, disordered eating patterns, gambling, spending money or overwork, as well as other problems.

All of these patterns have a negative effect on our lives. Our health, ability to pursue our life goals and meet our responsibilities may suffer. They also take a toll on our families through divorce or disruption of family life. They may interfere with our social or work relationships. They may also affect society in general, when we harm others, steal from them or create a societal need to deal with our addiction through the health or legal system.

Most people with addictions are quite good at denying anything is wrong with them. They can easily blame someone else or their bad luck. They may claim they can stop anytime they want, although they never seem to get around to it.

In most cases, there is something psychological behind our behavior. "I can talk to people better when I have a drink." "I will feel in control if I earn just a little more money." "People will like me if I am thin enough." We develop many false beliefs to justify our behavior and sometimes are not even aware of our own beliefs. We can actually convince ourselves to think there is something wrong with people who try to talk us out of our beliefs. Coming to terms with our addictive behavior means we also have to come to terms with our false beliefs. We can do it, but it is not easy.

FACING OUR ADDICTIONS

The next step after recognizing our addictions is facing them. They give us plenty of hints that something is wrong in our lives. Each time we receive a hint, we have the choice of taking it to heart or continuing to deny that anything is wrong and keep sliding further into the grip of our addiction.

There has been a considerable amount of controversy over the years about whether addiction is a disease. I used to think that looking at it as a disease was a cop-out. If it is a disease, I thought it implied there was nothing we could do about it. I have since learned that there is something we can do about any disease to give it less hold over our lives.

There is a book on dealing with alcoholism called *Loosening the Grip*. Being addicted means we are in the grip of behaviors that are destroying or diminishing our lives.

Loosening the grip seems like a good analogy to me. Dealing with an addiction is like prying a hand from around our neck one finger at a time. People who struggle with this process often say it is simple but not easy. Knowing what to do is clear, but following through and doing it can be quite a challenge.

It seems to me there are three steps to dealing with an addiction. The first step is to have a reason to stop. Until we become bothered enough, there is not much chance we will do anything about it. We need to reach the point of wanting back the parts of our lives which have been consumed.

The second step is doing something about it. There are many self-help books with strategies, including keeping a journal, substituting healthier behavior, stopping cold turkey, or tapering off. In my experience, I have found few people who make up their minds to get their lives under control and then do it on their own. Many people who are successful have the support of others who are dealing with the same or similar problem, such as AA or Weight Watchers. Others seek various forms of professional help.

There are people who have to start over, occasionally quite a few times, to finally be successful. There are also those who ultimately give up and decide it is too much trouble to change their behavior and slip back into old patterns.

The third step is addressing the underlying problems. Those of us who have trouble following through with our commitment, even with the help of others, have not dealt with the underlying problems which maintain our self defeating behavior. An informal study of patients at an eating disorder treatment agency found that the majority of patients arrived for treatment with severe depression and left with moderate depression. Even with the tools and support to battle their identified problem, there is still considerable emotional work to be done.

If we just address our addiction and not the underlying physical, emotional or spiritual lack in our lives, we stand on very precarious ground and remain at risk for slipping back into our old ways. Looking at the context of our addiction gives us a chance to refocus the rest of our life as well.

ADDICTIONS IN OUR LOVED ONES

Although we may never have struggled with addiction ourselves, most of us have loved ones who have been, or are in, the throes of such a war within themselves. I heard a radio commentary recently featuring a woman who made the point that her overeating and addiction to junk food were her business alone, did not hurt anyone else, and were not of concern to anyone else.

Unless they are self contained hermits, our loved ones certainly do affect those of us who care about them. We hear them complain about their addiction, see them struggle with the loss of part of their useful lives and are deprived of their company while they are being consumed by their problems. We can be drawn into helping with their legal entanglements, medical care or whatever efforts they make to become free of their addiction, or worse, see them decompensate while they maintain they are doing just fine.

When we have such loved ones in our lives, our first tendency may be to ignore or deny their difficulty, participating in their fantasy that there is no problem. We may blame others or maybe ourselves for their behavior, minimize it as not a big problem, or pretend with them that they can stop any time they want. None of these approaches are of any help and just encourage or worsen their situation.

Our first step is to be realistic and admit that we cannot control our loved ones' addictions. Nothing we can do will make them stop if they are not ready and willing to make some changes. That does not mean we should just give up.

The second step is to set boundaries. This means not allowing our loved ones' problems to destroy our lives, as well as theirs. Allowing them to ruin social occasions, drain us of money we need for other things or constantly complain to us about things they are not ready to change is not helpful to them or to us.

The third step is to let our loved ones know that we see them as addicted. This is a difficult step which must be done gently, but firmly and clearly. We must let them know we love them but do not accept what they are doing to themselves or to us. This is also a risky step, since they may choose their addiction over us, and cut off their relationship with us. They may leave us with the choice of wallowing in their misery with them or discontinuing our association with them for the time being.

Part of being effective with confrontation is choosing the right time to intervene. There may be a time when they are more open to our input, perhaps when the effect of their behavior on themselves or others is most obvious to them.

Once our loved ones recognize and make a commitment to dealing with their issues, there are many ways we can be supportive. Words or letters of encouragement can help. We may choose to go with them while they seek help or assist them in rebuilding their lives.

IT 'S NOT WHAT YOU EAT BUT WHAT'S EATING YOU

Why is eating such a problem for us and why is it so hard to manage? Looking back in our lives, food was one of the first comforts we received along with being held and having our diapers changed. There is some research to suggest that before age two, children have the ability to regulate what they eat and have a built in sense of their nutritional needs.

Some families criticize their young members as too skinny or too fat, leaving children feeling that changing their size will make them more acceptable. The same pattern follows children to school, where anyone the least bit different tends to be made fun of, size of body being an easy target. Adolescents sometimes find their food intake one of the few things they can easily control. Food becomes a symbol of what we want or don't want in our lives. It is not a matter of what we are eating but what is eating us.

Psychological issues come into play when we develop a pattern of eating much more than we need, eating much less or, in the case of bulimia, eat too much and then getting rid of the food by vomiting or using laxatives.

Even though people may engage in destructive eating patterns, they may feel they have little control over their behavior. This is the mystery of addictions. Patterns which look like decisions are made without much feeling of control on the part of the addict.

What is to be done? The first step is recognizing there is a problem. Health, job, and relationship concerns can all bring eating related problems to light, helping us to accept that there is a difficulty. People sometimes know at some level they have a problem, but are not quite ready to deal with it until a crisis arises.

The obvious next step is learning how to eat in a healthy way. Understanding what food means to us is another step. An obese person may not know how to develop a relationship and overeats as a way to find comfort from loneliness. An anorexic person may see life as quite out of control and finds restricting food as a way to take some control. A bulimic person may be looking for comfort and control and ends up bingeing.

Most of our emotions can be seen in the context of our relationships with other people. Some therapists have gone so far as to see feelings as having meaning only in the context of a relationship. Not only do we need to learn skills to manage our own thoughts and emotions, but we also need to find ways to negotiate relationships with people important in our lives.

None of this is easy to do. If it were, people would probably do it rather than suffer the distress of obesity and eating disorders. Many times it takes a team to deal with the nutritional, medical, psychiatric, psychological, and family/relationship issues.

FOOD, LIKE MONEY, BETTER A SERVANT THAN A MASTER

Life can go on without alcohol, tobacco or gambling. Twelve step addiction programs like AA point out that it is easier to get by without an addiction than it is to move from addiction to moderation. In this sense, getting over-eating under control is more difficult than managing other addictions. Food is still necessary for survival.

Figuring out how much to eat in order to raise, lower or maintain body weight is a simple matter of calculating the calories we burn compared to those we take in. Although quite logical, I would venture to say that this calculation plays a quite small part in the lives of the obese and holds a rather low priority.

Is obesity really about food? Packaged "diet" foods display their low fat or sugar percentages as if their use will solve the battle of the bulge. On the other hand, shame-lessly unhealthy food seems to predominate on the TV screen.

The problem with obesity is not what is going on in our stomachs but what is going on between our ears. Thoughts and feelings play a major part in becoming and staying obese.

"I ate those donuts because I was lonely." "Stopping on the way home for fast food took my mind off my frustration at work." "I was able to get back to sleep following an argument with my spouse after getting up for a midnight snack." Sound familiar?

Eating does nourish our bodies but can also help us deal with troublesome emotions, at least for the moment. Often it seems we do not have much control over our eating. Anger, sadness and frustration sometimes almost demand that we overeat. We are talking about a bad habit where we act without thinking.

There are alternatives. To change a habit, we must first stop to think about what we are doing. Once we realize what our pattern is, we can start to think about some alternatives. Keeping a record of what we eat and how we feel when we are eating helps sort out the pattern.

For example, once we realize we are overeating out of loneliness, we can think of other ways to be less lonely. Calling or visiting a friend, attending a community event or just going out to be around other people are more direct and useful ways of handling loneliness than feeling sorry for ourselves and seeking the temporary comfort of unneeded food.

Making a list of things we can do when we feel certain emotions can help us break the habit of turning to food to handle difficult times. One nutritionist I know suggested having a "comfort basket" filled with non-food comfort items.

A speaker at my church recently said that money makes a better servant than a master. The same is true of food.

Allowing it to take control of us makes it harder to manage and enjoy our lives. If we are in control, food can not only be useful but one of life's great pleasures.

CHAPTER 9

ADVERSITY

We all face troublesome times in our lives. We can allow these difficulties to crush us or learn how to use them to become stronger persons. This chapter addresses some of these troubles and some ideas about how to approach them.

RAGE AND ITS ALTERNATIVES

Have you tried passing a car on the Thruway only to find another car five feet from your back bumper? Have you tried to do something for a friend only to hear you are stupid for not doing it his way? For some people, annoyance can quickly escalate into rage.

Babies cry when they are uncomfortable but they cannot be said to be expressing rage. It seems clear that expressing rage is something we have to learn. Sometimes a family pattern dates back several generations. While there may be a few people affected in each generation, fortunately not all family members are tainted.

What is rage? The dictionary defines it as uncontrollable anger. Sometimes anger is justified. When we are wronged, being angry is appropriate. We have other ways to handle anger besides rage. We can express our anger directly to the one who had wronged us. We can explain how we feel in case the other person was unaware of how their behavior affected us. We can stop to consider our own reaction to see if our anger is justified.

Rage is letting our anger consume us to the extent that we lose control. We may get louder, often carrying on incoherently, dumping venom on our aggressor, or perhaps lashing out in a physical fury. Rage is generally an overreaction to a situation, out of proportion to how we have been treated.

How does rage develop? On the surface, it seems that someone does something we don't like and we react with rage. Actually, there is another step, one which takes place within us. We tell ourselves the other person had no right to do what he did. He is only doing it to upset us. If he had any sense, he would not do such a thing. We don't deserve what he did. We should not have to put up with him acting so stupid. He is so dense the only thing he could possibly understand is being blasted. Any of these thoughts sound familiar?

We can work ourselves into a rage quickly. If the above thoughts are familiar to us, it does not take much time to end up in a rage. Once we are in a rage, there is little we can do to change our reaction since rage is, by definition, uncontrollable anger.

We have two other choices. One is to avoid situations in which we know we are likely to go off the deep end. Unfortunately, we can't always predict when these will be. We can also think about what we tell ourselves when something happens to upset us. Is this person deliberately trying to upset us? Does he know we are likely to be upset? Could we explain how we feel in a milder way than rage?

We can also think about how good we are at sharing other emotions. If we don't know how to show embarrassment, fear, sorrow or loneliness, we may end up expressing all our negative emotions as rage. We can change this pattern, sometimes by talking with a friend, working with a counselor or taking an anger management course.

LONG TERM EFFECTS OF SEXUAL ABUSE

There are many opinions about how sexual abuse affects its victims. Thirty years ago sexual abuse was not discussed. Now talking about it does not have the stigma it once had.

The immediate effects are fairly clear most of the time. Children may have nightmares, anxiety, anger and depression. They may also have guilt feelings, sudden phobias, physical complaints, general fearfulness, withdrawal and feeling left out by others. Although any of these symptoms can be experienced by children, the sudden appearance of a number of these symptoms suggests the possibility of sexual abuse.

Children can come to feel the abuse is their fault if the perpetrator attempts to shift the blame by calling the child "seductive." The child may be seen by the perpetrator as wanting or at least agreeing to the abuse. If the abuse takes place in the family and the father is the abuser, the child may be blamed for breaking up the family when the father is required to leave for the safety of the child.

These short term effects are fairly well known. But what are the long term effects for adults who were sexually abused as children?

The most obvious effects are sexual. Adults who were sexually abused as children sometimes avoid intimate relationships or sometimes pursue them compulsively, hoping to make up for what happened in childhood. Many people with such experiences in their past find it difficult to maintain a relationship with a partner and get lost in feelings about the past. Having children often brings back feelings which were thought to have been resolved.

Eating disorders can be a result of sexual abuse. Sometimes food can be an attempt to find comfort and sometimes starvation can be a way to eliminate the outward signs of being female.

Adults who have been sexually abused as children tend to have lower self esteem than those who were not. Specifically, they tend to expect that things will not go well for them in life and that they have little control over what happens to them in their lives.

Women who have been sexually abused show higher rates of alcoholism. However, results of a number of studies have shown conflicting results in this area. More sophisticated studies have shown that sexually abused girls who also had mothers who were uncaring and overly controlling tend to have more difficulty with drinking. An important factor in recovery from sexual abuse is how mothers treat their daughters. Maternal support can make recovery much easier.

Depression and anxiety are other difficulties more common with adults who have been sexually abused. These are not surprising findings, given the betrayal of childhood trust accompanying sexual abuse of a child.

Running through all of these difficulties is the lack of self confidence and trust of others which are important in so many areas of life. Although all of this sounds rather dire, sexual abuse as a child does not condemn a person to a life of misery.

RECOVERY FROM SEXUAL ABUSE

Recovery from sexual abuse is not a simple process. Just admitting it happened is shameful for the victim, the family and anyone associated with the perpetrator. Nevertheless, facing it is the first step. Sometimes the memory is buried and is uncovered in layers, almost like an onion. It may begin with having an uncomfortable feeling that something happened and then gradually becoming aware of the specifics.

For others, the memory is graphically fixed in their mind and surfaces at the most inconvenient times. It is always just below the surface and can be triggered by intimacy, a doctor's appointment, a movie or just about anything related to sex.

Most sexual abuse victims say it would help tremendously if the perpetrator took responsibility for what happened. Knowing their abuser takes responsibility for what happened is somewhat of a relief. This may also be a first step in the abuser making some changes and possibly reducing the chances of his abusing someone else.

The abuser taking responsibility also means the victim has less reason to keep the secret. Child victims are often seduced or threatened into feeling it is their responsibility to protect everyone by keeping the secret.

Having a supportive mother is also quite helpful. Long term effects of sexual abuse are less severe for girls whose mothers are supportive. What would it be like to tell your mother you were abused and then have her tell you to stop making up lies? It seems hard to imagine but it does happen. It is more common in families where a mother may have been sexually abused as a child herself and is reluctant to admit she has married someone who abuses her daughter, or is afraid of what will happen to the family if her husband is removed.

A supportive mother can protect her daughter from further abuse and help her feel cherished and valuable. A child is not equipped to wade alone through all the confusing thoughts and emotions accompanying sexual abuse.

As an adult, a loving, patient, understanding sexual partner can help a person with a sexual abuse history learn to feel normal about herself or himself. Unfortunately people who have distorted views about themselves tend to attract partners who have their own warped ideas about sexuality and relationships.

Counseling and various therapy approaches can be quite helpful on a number of fronts. People with a sexual abuse history need to learn how to feel physically and emotionally safe, to learn that the abuse was not their fault and to learn to take control of their lives. Support groups with other sexual abuse survivors can help participants feel normal again.

Resolution of issues with the perpetrator is helpful but not always possible. The perpetrator can take responsibility for his actions. The victim can also forgive the molester. This does not mean what he did was okay. It means that the victim can learn to let go of anger which can be emotionally consuming and get on with her life.

A CLOSE SHAVE

He had been assigned to sea duty and was stationed on a small tanker which served submarines. He had been trained as a pharmacist's mate and after promotion to ensign, was transferred to the tanker.

He did not know what happened until the next morning. The Second World War was raging, and ships appeared to be everywhere in the Pacific. The harbor at Guam was not designed for American warships. There was not enough room for the many submarines and tenders to dock. To accommodate all the warships, they were docked side to side, known as rafting, and looking like so many sausages in a row. The tankers tied up next to the submarines to fuel them, while provisions were also brought on board.

As an ensign, Joe had access to the communications room. As he passed the communications bench, he noticed a confidential memo. On 01 July at 1526 hours, a torpedo had been dropped during the loading of submarine 030. The memo was to all captains, alerting them to the need for caution in handling torpedoes. Joe realized that one exploding torpedo could ignite the rest of the torpedoes on the submarine. One exploding submarine might well destroy all the other subs to say nothing of the tankers.

The number of the sub seemed familiar to Joe. He had never been in one and did not relish the thought. He did wonder what it must be like to be under water in such a delicate shell. Worst of all must be the knowledge that you were under attack. He had talked with submariners about the terror of hearing depth charges explode next to your hull. And those were the survivors of attacks. What must it have been like in the last moments of a hopelessly leaking submarine? What Joe had not considered was that a submarine carried the means of its own destruction in its torpedo rooms.

He walked out of the communications room with these thoughts. It was time for his break. He decided to climb to the bridge where there was some breeze. When he reached the bridge, he looked at the submarine docked next to his ship. He happened to look at the conning tower and noticed the sub's number. It was 030.

There were probably other close calls he had not known about and he was just as glad not to. Life was precious. There was no way to know how much longer he would live but he would be sure to savor whatever time he had left.

This story was told to me by my father about his experience in World War II. It made me think that war may well have prevented me from being born if the incident had turned out different. My children and grandchildren would not have been born. I also think about the people dying in the war in Iraq and wonder about the lives and possibilities which will not be realized because of the terror of war and it makes me sad.

SORT OF STUCK

Jesse felt life was hopeless. Her husband whistled out the door every morning on his way to work. Her three children got out of bed, dressed, ate breakfast and made it to the bus on time, at least most mornings.

She got up before the rest of her family, made the coffee and put the cereal on the table. Her house buzzed with activity for a short time until everyone else was out the door. She watched them go merrily on their way. This morning she looked in the mirror when she was alone and saw a middle aged woman in an old bathrobe with semi-ratty hair. She didn't look very happy either.

Jesse thought of her fifteen year old daughter, Lisa. Clean scrubbed, crisp blouse, face aglow, she bounded out the door with the excitement of greeting the world for another day. Jesse realized it could have been her eighteen years ago. It was hard to remember being that enthusiastic about life. In some ways it seemed only yesterday. Too much had happened over the years.

Her mother had developed cancer when Jesse was sixteen, just a year older than Lisa was now. Dance lessons had to stop. Jesse was suddenly baby-sitting for her younger brother and sister, and it was not clear for a while whether her mother would live. Her father relied on her heavily, making it clear he did not like having to do so.

Her mother stabilized after two years, but Jesse felt she had lost touch with her teenage self. She did get some satisfaction from helping her parents with the younger children and eventually came to feel helping was her main job in life.

She had not thought much about this, but it seemed most of the young men she dated were pretty needy and she easily adapted to their needs. Some of them commented on how she appreciated the small things and how little it took to please her. She eventually became close to Vance who accepted her as she was and seemed to have few expectations of her.

Vance was a klutz. He always seemed to lose things or forget arrangements he and Jesse had made. She was annoyed sometimes but told him it was no big deal. She decided she could help him become more responsible but knew it would be a long term project. The marriage sealed her commitment to reform him. He knew nothing of her project. Vance went blithely on his way with Jesse close behind, mending fences and picking up the pieces of his chaotic life. As the children came along, she added their care to her duties, not expecting much from Vance since he had enough trouble trying to keep organized.

How had the face in the mirror changed from her daughter's brightness to the drawn pastiness she saw looking back at her without much enthusiasm?

Jesse did not know how she had become depressed. After a while in therapy she might have realized how it developed. She had to grow up very quickly and had adult responsibilities dropped on her just as she was starting to be ready to make some of her own choices. She did not have time to think about what she might want from life. She learned to be a people pleaser and forgot her own needs. She accepted this as her lot in life and did not learn she could ask for what she wanted. She did not realize that taking responsibility for others kept them from becoming responsible for themselves.

Jesse was at a turning point. Prozac might make her feel better for a while. Complaining to friends might help her feel others understood how she was sacrificing herself. Leaving her husband might help her feel relieved for a while until she found someone else to take care of.

If she is alert, Jesse may notice some of the opportunities in her life to make some changes. A friend might give her a copy of *Codependent No More*, suggesting it was okay for her to have a life of her own. She might talk with her husband about her resentment over taking care of him and suggest they work together to help him start taking care of himself. She might join a friend at a health club a couple nights a week while her husband watches the kids.

Some people are happy to meet everyone else's needs but they always seem to have something like chronic health problems suggesting all is not well. Depression is giving in to a hopeless situation. The way out for Jesse is to realize it is hopeless only because she thinks it is. She may need to begin realizing she has choices and then decide on a course which does not leave her stuck. That will be the beginning of her way out of depression.

WHERE DOES STRESS COME FROM?

Many people these days complain of stress. People go on disability due to post traumatic stress disorder. Our children, work and others' expectations of us can all be sources of stress. One dictionary defines stress as "a mentally or emotionally disruptive or disquieting influence." This is the sixth listed meaning. The first is listed as "importance, significance or emphasis placed on something." The meaning in physics is "an applied force that tends to strain or deform a body."

What do we mean by stress? Usually we refer to something which bothers us. There are many degrees of stress from mild annoyance to feeling overwhelmed. Stress is understood more from our reaction to it than from what is actually happening to us. Our circumstances also influence how we experience a stressful incident. If everything is going well, we may take a fairly large stress in stride. If everything is going wrong, an otherwise minor stress may put us over the edge.

What about the other definitions of stress listed above? The first definition refers to importance, significance or emphasis. Something can stand out without being particularly good or bad. In music or in speaking, a phrase can be stressed, making it stand out from its surroundings with no particular value judgments or feelings involved.

The definition from physics hits a little closer to home. A body is strained or deformed. It is easy to imagine strain on a bridge joint when a train rolls across a trestle. There are similar results from our stress. We can feel run down or tense under stress. We can also develop ulcers, hypertension or, in the extreme, waste away from malnutrition or gorge ourselves until obesity is a major problem. It seems like stress just happens and we react. Like many things in life, it is not quite that simple. There certainly are stressful situations in our lives and we certainly have a variety of stress reactions. Stress starts with what happens to us and ends up affecting us emotionally or physically.

Two things affect our reaction to stress. One is the circumstance under which the stress occurs. If the stressful situation in question is the only one we face all week, it is not so bad. If we have ten stressful situations to deal with at once, it is a different story.

Sometimes we have little control over the number of stressors we have to face at any given time. Maybe it's just bad luck. Sometimes we have more control over our stressors and contribute to our own stress. For example, the stress of a high mortgage, car payment and credit card bills comes from our choice of how to live. We could have chosen to live in a way which did not involve those stresses.

The other factor affecting our response to stress is our thinking. We do not often stop to examine this part of our stress. We are thinking all the time, even when we are sleeping, and tend to take our thinking for granted. We do not think about our thinking very much. Whether we are aware of it or not, our thinking has a considerable effect on how we react to a stressful situation.

Consider an example. Suppose you are walking down the street and someone bumps into you. Do you get upset? If you see this person bumping into everyone in front of you on purpose and laughing, you would probably get quite angry. If the person is distracted by a conversation, and is not watching where he is going, you might get less angry. If the person is carrying a white cane and obviously can't see you, how angry would you get?

The same thing happens in each case, you get bumped. However, you may well have three different reactions depending on how you see the circumstances and what you tell yourself about them.

Some of us get in the habit of talking ourselves into reacting in quite negative ways. Some of us also tend to take things personally. We sometimes think people are doing things to us rather than just doing them.

If you stop to think about it, most of the things we do are for our own reasons rather than because of what someone else does or thinks. Even if we think we are reacting to someone else's behavior, it is more a reaction to what we tell ourselves about their behavior than to how they act. We can become angry if we feel slighted by someone regardless of whether they even know we feel slighted.

We can choose to avoid some of our stress by choosing not to allow it in our lives or taking others' actions less personally. Stress can be easier to manage if we find a different way to think about it. We always have choices, even if they are not the ones we would like at the time.

How have we come to feel so much stress these days? I think part of the answer lies in cultural changes. Two hundred years ago, people struggled for survival and had little time to stop and think what their lives were like. I am not sure life was any less stressful then, but people took for granted the stress of life.

We have grown used to the convenience of home appliances to lessen our work and rely on medications for every discomfort. We don't expect to have to deal with stress and are surprised when it hits us between the eyes. We forget that stressful situations are a part of life, that we have some control over these situations and that we have choices about how to react to our stress. Next time you are feeling under stress, think about how you got there and concentrate less on how awful it is and more on what you can do about it.

CREATIVE STRESS

When I first started in the mental health field in the early 1970's, there was not much talk of stress. Hans Selye's book, *The Stress of Life*, was still fairly new. His theory was that stress, unattended, took a toll on the body and eventually led to a breakdown at vulnerable points and led to various physical conditions. His theory has been debated over the years but now it is commonly accepted that stress takes its toll on the body.

There was a time when doctors would tell their patients, "Its all in your head" when they couldn't find a physical explanation for a complaint. Sometimes there are very elusive diseases, almost impossible to detect. Sometimes life pressures can be overwhelming. If left to build, they result in physical disorders. Hypertension, obesity, eating disorders and addictions, to name a few, can be the end result of stress beyond our ability to cope.

Battle fatigue has long been known to be a psychological stress reaction to the horrors of war. The more recent term, Post Traumatic Stress Disorder, has come to include lasting reactions to traumatic events such as rape, assault or even witnessing such events. Treatment of stress has become a big time industry.

There are plenty of approaches to dealing with stress. Vacations are a way of getting away from life stressors. Meditation, exercise, massage, assertiveness training, cognitive behavior therapy and medication are some of the more recent approaches to dealing with stress.

But what is stress? Most people think they know it if they see it or feel it, but it is not so easy to define. The dictionary calls stress "a physical, chemical or emotional factor that caused bodily or mental tension." Selye sees stress as "the state manifested by a specific syndrome which consists of all the nonspecifically induced changes within a biologic system." That's quite a mouthful.

Unless you go on to define all the terms Selye uses, this definition seems more confusing than helpful. It is hard to put your life work in a few words as Selye tried to do. What I think Selye is saying is that stress is the reaction of the body to anything that upsets our internal apple cart. He has studied bodily changes in response to stress. While we generally notice things like headaches, upset stomach, muscle pain or difficulty sleeping, Selye has shown that the whole body reacts to stress. He talks about three steps of response to stress: alarm, or being alert to the intruder, resistance, or fighting back, and exhaustion, or giving in to the stress. How well we cope with stress depends on our inherited coping ability, our diet and how we have coped with stress in the past.

Peter Hanson, in *Stress for Success*, lists events which most people find stressful. Some stressors are fairly obvious such as death of a spouse, death of a close family member, divorce, or a jail term. Some stressors are not so obvious. These include marriage, retirement, marital reconciliation, change in financial state (not necessarily for the worse) and outstanding personal achievement. Some stressors may be a bit of a surprise such as a change in living conditions, a change in recreation, having a mortgage less than one year's salary, a change in eating habits, a vacation or Christmas.

We usually think of stress as something negative, to be avoided or managed. However, studies of people taking examinations have shown that people feeling high levels of stress or low levels of stress do not do as well as people with moderate levels of stress. Maybe stress is not all bad.

But can stress be a positive force? Peter Hanson talks about learning to manage our response to stress rather than trying to eliminate it. He talks about stress in a range from boredom to panic. People are not usually very productive at either extreme. We can try to eliminate stress by avoiding stressful situations altogether, usually resulting in boredom. Using drugs and alcohol to blot out our feeling of stress usually leaves us closer to panic when the effect wears off and the stress is still there.

How can we use stress in a creative way in our lives? Selye talked about the importance of our preparation for stress. Physical fitness and good nutrition prepare our bodies for the onslaught of stress. Mental conditioning can prepare us emotionally and mentally. Having an understanding of what our lives are about and why we are here on earth gives us a context in which to handle the adversity of stress. Stress can begin to be viewed as a challenge rather than another load we have to carry.

How do we make this change? Napoleon Hill said that "every adversity carries within it the seeds of an at least equivalent benefit." We can start looking at the challenge presented to us by a particular stress rather than focusing on the burden it presents. What makes us react to stress in a positive or negative way? Daniel Goleman in *Emotional Intelligence*, sees our sense of control of our lives as critical. Seeing our lives as out of control, leads to feeling overwhelmed, threatened, paralyzed or demoralized. He talks of the quality of hardiness as "the ability to stay committed, feel in control and be challenged rather than threatened by stress."

How do we get this feeling of control in our lives? On the physical level, fitness and nutrition keep our body prepared to withstand stress which might otherwise lead to irritability, ulcers or maybe even a heart attack. Relaxation exercises can help us keep our level of stress away from the extreme of panic.

Emotionally, staying in balance with those around us helps us maintain a support system of people who care about us and who can be there when stress tries to knock us off balance.

Intellectually we can learn to think about stress in a different way than we might have in the past. Actually, it is the way we think about stress, rather than what actually happens, that upsets us. We have a choice of how we look at events in our lives and do not have to focus on the tragedy. We can think of our situation as unfair and focusing on "why me?" We can think about what challenge the situation presents, and how we can use it to better ourselves.

Spiritually we can stop feeling sorry for ourselves and start thinking about how we can find a benefit in it for ourselves and for others. How can this stressful situation make me a better person? This last aspect of handling stress may be the most difficult. Let's consider an example. A man loses his business, family and friends due to his alcoholism. He can wallow in these losses, blame the world, and continue deeper into his drinking. His other choice is to use his losses as a lesson, find the supports he needs to stop drinking and keep it under control, eventually using what he has learned to help others deal with their drinking. Not easy to do, but possible.

None of the things we have talked about, nutrition, fitness, relaxation, building relationships, changing our thinking or way of looking at life are easy. They are all possible with some effort and can be the building blocks of creative stress.

THE MESSAGE OF ILLNESS

Recently I was knocked flat on my back with pneumonia for over a week. I have often wondered what the point of illness was. On the surface of it, there does not appear to be any earthly reason for being sick. It is hard to think of anything good about lying in bed feeling miserable.

I had to put on hold all the things I thought were important. I had too much to do to be sick and being laid up was a great waste of time. People were depending on me. Who would do the things I had planned? How would the world go on without me?

It is easy to be angry about being sick. It is definitely a pain in the neck or some other part of one's anatomy. Important work does not get done. I am not good for much if someone I care about needs something. There is no point even considering social plans.

As I lay in bed, all of these thoughts running through my head, I tried to make sense of being sick. In the midst of all this, the quiet voice of my wise friend, Steve, whispered to me in my mind. I don't remember his exact words, but he once said that illness is a sign from God that there is something in your life you might need to consider changing.

I think God has many such messages for us on a daily basis. But we are too busy to notice them as we bustle along, trying to keep up with all the things we think are important, seldom stopping to think what our lives are really about. Since I wasn't going anywhere and could not focus on anything else, even writing, all I could do was entertain Steve's comment. What is it I need to change in my life? I am doing well with my work, my writing is coming along, I am helpful to people when I can be and I have been enjoying life. What was missing?

A few things came to mind. I have gotten so busy that I have not been exercising or paying much attention to my nutrition. Grinding to a halt with illness, not being able to exercise or eat, made me aware of my neglect of my body. Although I have been moving toward my writing goals, I don't do it consistently and spend a fair amount of time passively watching TV or mindlessly wandering around the WEB with no particular purpose. The message of my illness was that I could take better care of my body and stay more focused on the goals I see as important. I am now recuperating with a renewed sense of what my priorities are. I also learned that I need to take the time on a daily basis to pay attention to the subtle messages from God, rather than having to wait for a divine kick in the butt.

GO GENTLE INTO THAT
GOOD NIGHT

Dylan Thomas wrote a poem with the opposite title, "Do not go gentle into that good night." His poem focused on wrestling with death, a tooth and nail struggle with the end of life.

None of us wants to die unless we are feeling overwhelmed by pain and sickness, experiencing problems which seem to get worse no matter what we do, or seeing ourselves as too old and worn out to go on. People in these circumstances are resigned to death and are willing to let go.

It seems to me that how we approach death depends on

how we approach life. If we view life as a competition with others, death may be the final contest to see who can live the longest. If we view life as a joy ride, we will fight to get all we can from it. If we view life as a gift from God, death is the final part of the journey. We often hear talk of someone dying before their time, or what a waste it is that a person died so young. How do we understand a baby's death?

My sense is that God gives each of us a certain amount of life as a gift, for some people a very short time and for some much longer. We are not entitled to any life at all and are here on earth to make the best use of what we are given according to God's plan and request of us. We are not God and have no way of knowing why some people are given so little life and some so much. Our job is to use well what we have.

No one knows what lies ahead after death or whether there is an afterlife. I dare say none of us has met anyone who has come back with a report from the other side of the grave. Most cultures believe in an afterlife, making our efforts on earth worthwhile and giving us the basis for an eternal reward. Hindus believe that if we do not get it right the first time, we get to come back in another incarnation to try again.

Even though we cannot know what lies beyond the grave, our faith in God draws us to believe there is a heavenly reward awaiting us. If there were no God, there would not be much point in living a moral life.

Belief in a loving God with the promise of eternal life allows us a peaceful acceptance of death as a transition to a higher plane. Skeptics will say there is no proof that anything lies beyond. George Bernard Shaw, the playwright and notorious agnostic, when asked, said that when he dies, if there is a God, they will sit down and talk about it man to man. We don't have to wait until we die, but can sit down and talk with God right now about our life and death. May the angels lead us into Paradise.

LESSONS FROM A FUNERAL

Recently, I attended the funeral of a person I did not know well. He was close to people I did know, which is the reason I was at the funeral. To some extent I was able to relate to the grief of his family, particularly during the funeral, where it was most visible. Since I was not that close to him, I was also able to think about the whole funeral process and put it into perspective for myself.

Michael did not die an old man, but had suffered with cancer for some time and became quite incapacitated in his last days, although his sense of humor stayed with him to the end. Invariably I have heard things in eulogies I never knew about the deceased. That was not surprising in this case, since I did not really know him. However I have also found surprises in eulogies of my aunts and uncles whom I thought I knew fairly well. I was surprised to learn some things about my father from the reflection on his life I undertook in writing his eulogy.

It seems everyone's life ends up being about something, whether it is a series of accomplishments, overcoming adversity or, as in the case of my grandfather, showing the rest of us how to live in peace and joy.

Michael's life turned out to be about coming to terms with his wild side, being true to his convictions and approaching adversity with a sense of humor.

Comments I have heard at funerals include, "She had a full life," or, "It was a shame he died so young." I have finally come to realize that no one is guaranteed any amount of life and never dies too soon, except from the perspective of those left behind. Everyone has a certain amount of time, although no one knows for sure how much. It is up to each of us to make the best of the time we have.

We are all on earth for a purpose and have something we can leave behind for those who follow us. The lesson of our life can enrich those whose lives we have touched.

There is a bumper sticker which reads, "He who dies with the most toys wins." I guess that may be true if we want to be remembered for our toys, all of which will end up in someone else's possession when we die. None of us knows how much time we have been allotted. If we want to leave something else as our legacy, it would behoove us to figure out what we want to leave as our legacy and get working on it.

CHAPTER 10

EVIL

Some experiences in life go beyond being difficult and reach the point of being evil. Facing, understanding, and coping with evil are the focus of this chapter.

THE MYSTERY OF EVIL

Did you ever wonder why there is evil in the world? What is evil, really? It is not easy to define. One medieval definition describes evil as the absence of good. Good isn't so easy to define either. We all seem to have a sense of what evil means to us even though it might be hard to put into words. The dictionary defines evil as "the fact of suffering, misfortune and wrongdoing, a cosmic evil force or something that brings sorrow, distress or calamity."

Some Muslim leaders have referred to our country as the evil enemy of their religion. Our president has called several countries an Axis of Evil. When you get right down to it, evil means something we detest and see as a threat to our way of life. How can two different ways of life both be evil? Is one way right and the other way wrong? Could it be that people with different views of life think they alone are right and others wrong? Being different does not make beliefs right or wrong.

I remember attending a Catholic elementary school. Across the street was a public school we referred to as the "Protestant School" although Catholic, Jewish and perhaps other religious views as well as Protestant were represented. Looking back, it is easy to see that we saw ourselves as righteous, just and saved while those across the street were ignorant, wrong and doomed. Children usually think in black and white terms. People are either good or bad, nice or nasty, smart or dumb. There is no room for shades of gray or distinctions. Everything is clear cut.

As we mature, hopefully we find things are not quite as simple as we thought. People can do bad things but have some good qualities, although it is still easy to think of people in global terms without making distinctions. When I taught college courses at Attica Correctional Facility, I was warned not to tell people I was teaching there because many thought it was a waste of time. They also thought prisoners did not deserve an education. I discovered that among my students, some were in class to avoid boredom. Some were just curious. Some really wanted to make changes in their lives. There were shades of gray like any college program.

Being different from us does not mean being evil. People with very different religious or political views from our own still have dreams they pursue, families they love and children they cherish, just as we do. They may have the same goals we do although they have a different way of pursuing or expressing them.

From what I can tell, there is no easy way to get beyond our prejudices and see the good in other people who seem very different from us. Perhaps the challenge of living in a diverse world is to find a way to meet our life goals while seeing the good in those different from ourselves and helping them pursue their own goals in their own way.

THE REALITY OF EVIL

I wrote before about how people who are different from us can appear evil, especially if they seem to threaten our way of life. Ways of living or behaving are not necessarily evil because they differ from our way of doing things. But are there actions or people we can all agree are evil?

Harming or even killing someone without reason seems to qualify. Rape, theft, and deceit are others. Sometimes it is hard for us to bring ourselves to see particularly heinous crimes as evil. We instead say it must take a truly sick individual to do such a thing. We are suggesting that we can't imagine acting this way on purpose. Some people are referred to as animals since it is hard to accept their behavior as human. For something to be evil, not only must the behavior be seen as bad but the perpetrators must be seen as choosing to act the way they do. Choosing to act in an evil way must be clearly understood as harmful to another person yet still done deliberately. Accidents are not seen as evil.

In most states, we do not execute people who are retarded or mentally ill. We take the position that criminals must both understand what they are doing and make a free choice to commit their crimes anyway. In other states, we seem to punish perpetrators regardless of their ability to understand what they are doing or to form intent.

In cases where we deem acts evil, but do not view the perpetrators as acting rationally, more enlightened communities usually choose to protect society by incarcerating them in a mental hospital until they are of sound mind and no longer considered dangerous. We do not see them as deliberately choosing evil but nevertheless they remain dangerous.

There are also individuals we consider inherently evil. They have committed either a long string of crimes or a crime of such magnitude that we as a society cannot bring ourselves to trust them again. We see them as choosing evil and not likely to make any significant change in their ability to maker better choices.

Punishment of such people is usually motivated by society's revenge, since the likelihood of rehabilitation is remote at best. Evil people find a way to be evil even in prison. Society's best motivation for removal of evil people from general circulation is self protection from further assaults.

There have been studies of evil people suggesting hereditary, social, economic and personal experiences as factors in turning people evil. As far as I know there is yet to be a good explanation of why two people with nearly identical parents and life experiences can turn out very different, one corrupted by his or her experiences and another surviving them and being purified by them. Evil remains a mystery in our world, sometimes a desperate choice, sometimes deliberate infliction of pain and sometimes with no explanation at all.

RESPONDING TO EVIL

I think most of us have heard about the three monkeys, one covering its ears, one its eyes and one its mouth with the motto, "Hear no evil, see no evil, speak no evil."

We would all like to live in a world with no evil, and would prefer not to notice or acknowledge its presence among us. The reality is that evil, at least occasionally, touches the lives of us all and brings us to the point where we must acknowledge it.

What can we do about evil? What are our choices? If we are touched closely enough and severely enough, our initial response might be to try to stomp out the evildoer or have someone do it for us. I dare say most of us have at least had a passing thought of killing someone who has brought evil into our lives. We might entertain a biblical response, "an eye for an eye." Evildoers deserve to have done to them whatever they have done to us. More rarely, and usually after time for us to heal, we may offer forgiveness to the evildoer.

It would be nice if it were otherwise, but the sad fact is that punishment does not usually have any impact on serious evildoers except to confirm their disregard for others and increases their angry response to whatever they do not like in society. While it might make us feel better, punishment usually has little if any positive effect on criminals and generally does not deter others from similar criminal acts. Keeping evildoers out of circulation until they are ready to behave does make society safer even though it comes at a fairly high price financially.

What was that about forgiveness? Could this even be an option? We have all heard victims or their relatives pledge angrily, " I will never forgive him (or her) for what he (or she) did." Have you ever stopped to think whether a criminal who has wronged you really cares how you feel while you remain angry years later?" If you are the one who made the pledge and you stick with it, your face is the one contorted in anger and your life is disrupted by clinging to your rage.

There are different kinds of forgiveness. One is to say that what the evildoer did was okay and you will forget about it. This is not the kind of forgiveness I mean. Of course it isn't okay, and you will never forget being touched by evil.

The kind of forgiveness I mean is letting go of your anger and your focus on revenge. God and society will have plenty of consequences for the evildoer without your personal involvement. You can do what you can to see that you, your loved ones and society are safe from further assaults. Then you can return your focus to living the best life you can rather than allowing yourself to continue being consumed by another's evil.

TOWARD UNDERSTANDING AND
TREATING THE MOLESTER

A number of recent articles have appeared in the news about priests molesting children. Although priests have been in the news lately, they are not the only ones who molest children. Parents, neighbors, coaches and others have abused their power advantage to ensnare children. Responsibility for what happens is never the child's, despite what some molesters maintain.

For some, the lack of a loving partner may exaggerate their loneliness. Celibacy may be a further complicating factor for Catholic priests who end up molesting children. Celibacy may also be a hiding place for those lacking the ability to form an intimate relationship. Either of these difficulties may make approaching children sexually more of a risk.

It is very difficult to look beyond this behavior to gain an understanding of what motivates it. Our first reaction as a society is outrage and our response is to want to incarcerate and punish the offenders. If they do get paroled, we would like them to be clearly labeled. Perhaps the scarlet letter could be brought back.

There is little general interest in understanding these people or how they might be helped in treatment. We tend to think of their behavior as a deliberate choice for which they should be punished. Is there a way to understand and perhaps change this behavior? While some are "predatory pedophiles," as former priest John Geogan was described, studies suggest that others are often arrested in their development around adolescence. In other words, they never become adults emotionally. The theory is that they suffer emotional trauma in their childhood which prevents them from developing adult emotions. They tend to be on the same emotional level as the children they try to engage.

Physical, emotional or sexual abuse leaves them feeling worthless and incapable of being loved by other adults. They tend to be attracted by the innocence of childhood and in a distorted way feel that a child could accept them when they have no chance of an adult relationship.

In their desperation, for love and acceptance, they have little understanding of the emotional harm they inflict on the children they approach, often the same emotional pain they experienced when they were abused as children. Their behavior is addictive although they are still responsible for it as alcoholics are for their alcohol addiction.

The first step, a big one, is to admit their behavior is a problem. Without this, no change is possible. The next step is to work toward a better acceptance of themselves, learning to feel worthwhile as people. Developing and practicing social skills is the next step in working toward healthy adult relationships. None of this is easy or quickly accomplished. Years of treatment may be required.

During the process, probation or parole supervision helps offenders maintain boundaries difficult to maintain on their own. This approach does not work for all sexual offenders, but it is possible for at least some to learn more responsible behavior.

CHAPTER 11

PERSONAL REFLECTIONS

This chapter includes some observations about events in my life. Although not unique, they show how I have attempted to use what I have learned to manage and understand some of my experiences.

TURNING SIXTY

Last week a wonderful party surprised me for my sixtieth birthday. I had no idea what was afoot until I walked in the door, wondering what my mother, brothers and sister were doing at a party I was led to believe had nothing to do with me. It took me a while to realize what was going on.

As I thought about the party, I realized I was just as surprised to be sixty years old as I was to find myself at the party. I have had sixty years to get ready for this event, but still it snuck up on me. I still can't bring myself to use the word "old" when I think of myself.

I thought a little about how I arrived at this point in my

life. Part of it was just by staying alive long enough. Even that can't be taken for granted. I remember when I was first learning to drive, I passed another car on a curve and survived by the skin of my teeth. I was lucky to live through adolescence.

I have often wondered how much control I have had over the direction of my life. When I was seven, I remember a bedtime conversation with my mother about the possibilities in life. I wanted to be a priest and a doctor which my mother thought was possible. I spent a fair amount of time in the seminary without actually becoming a priest. I also became a doctor, but a psychologist rather than a physician as I had expected.

I wondered too about the people who have come through my life. Some of them just happened to inhabit the places I frequented, such as school, church and work. Other people I met through sports, literary activities or social events. The real surprises came in meeting people again whom I knew in a previous context, such as the bartender who remembered me as his hockey coach when he was ten.

Perhaps most surprising have been the side roads I have taken, which ended up being whole new avenues. I think of Frost's poem, "The Road Not Taken" and wonder how many unexplored possibilities have lain in the shadows of the paths I have taken and how many hidden opportunities there are in each of our lives. I also think of the experiences which still await me. I sometimes wonder what I will do when I grow up.

Life is a great adventure, approached with the mind of a child. Children do not have any preconceptions about life.

They take each experience as it is presented and don't distort their perceptions by prejudices. Did you ever watch a child at the beach discover a sand crab? The child looks in fascination as the crab skitters sideways and reveals its few secrets. The child watches in awe. I don't want to stay stuck in childhood like Peter Pan in Neverland, but I do always want to approach each new adventure with an open mind and watch its mysteries unfold.

THE GIFT OF PROSPERITY

Have you ever thought about what prosperity really means. The government and the news media tell us about lower unemployment, higher wages and the ability to buy more things or spend more on vacations. It is as if a dollar amount can measure prosperity. But do money or things make us prosperous? Was Howard Hughes prosperous? Maybe on paper. I have come to see prosperity as a state of mind rather than of the wallet or bank account.

I would like to share my journey toward prosperity. My father worried all his life about whether he would have too little money to provide for us, whether he would lose his job or whether he would be poor in retirement. None of these things happened and he always had enough money although he always worried about it. My mother inherited from her parents a healthy respect for money, provided well for us and taught us to respect our money and possessions. We were exposed to two opposing views of money and wealth.

At age thirteen I entered the Catholic seminary and began

to learn about the vow of poverty. No one owned things in the seminary but we held things in common or had more personal things set aside for our individual use. No one worried about whether "mine is better than yours" and we all learned a healthy respect for community property.

When I left the seminary at age twenty three, I had to take care of myself for the first time in my life. I had two hundred dollars to my name and no immediate prospects for any more money. I borrowed money for college and living expenses and married without much thought as to where I would find the money to support my family. I bought or charged what I thought I needed, expecting my future income to bail me out.

I managed to increase my debt, sometimes for legitimate reasons, sometimes not. I thought I had to rely on myself. I concentrated on getting more money and not letting what I had get away from me. I clung tight to my money, hoping to survive. The closer I gripped my little bit of wealth, the more it seemed to slip through my fingers.

I started making some changes, but too late. My marriage ended and I found myself bankrupt. I learned from others' experience that bankruptcy could be only a temporary halt to a downward spiral. I knew if I went along the same way I had in the past, I would probably end up in a worse situation. I learned from others it was best to avoid debt and live on a cash basis. This sounded good, but I still had debts and struggled to survive on a daily basis.

Then two things happened to change my life. I met a woman who knew how to live simply, within her means and without attachment to things. She was also generous with her money. In addition, my brother introduced me to Unity Church were I first heard about a spiritual interpretation of prosperity. This idea baffled me at first. I thought prosperity meant being wealthy and not having to worry about money.

I tried to make logical sense of prosperity as I had been trained to do in graduate school. Still, I had no idea how I could pay what I saw as overwhelming maintenance after my divorce, but started writing the word "prosperity" on all my maintenance checks and thought of them as my contribution to the circulation of the wealth of the universe. I doubled what I thought was a comfortable amount to donate to church and looked for ways my money or possessions could benefit others more than me. I was wary at first, but soon found myself enjoying more what I had and worrying less about where the money I needed would come from.

I found myself back in the spirit of my former vow of poverty where things and money are part of God's universe and came my way for my temporary use and enjoyment. I found I could enjoy things much more when I was not clinging to them.

I had come to see prosperity not as related to the state of my bank account, car, house or what I could afford to do. For me, prosperity is living in balance with the riches of God's universe, giving what I can to help others live their lives and enjoying in a non-possessive way the riches coming in my direction.

I still think it is necessary to work hard, make plans and be organized. But worrying about the future does not help. There are constructive things we can do about the future, but worrying about it is not one of them. With an open mind, I will see what is necessary to do and what is in my best interest.

Hopefully the story of my journey will be of some help to you in considering your own course.

Here are some things I have learned about prosperity:

1. Approach the abundance of the world with reverence. It is here to enjoy but not to worship or cling to.

2. Prosperity requires priming the pump. No water comes up from a well unless some is first sent down the well to get it started.

3. We need a balance of trust and responsibility for the future. While it is useless to fret about the future, it is our job to make reasonable plans.

4. Random acts of kindness are contagious. If we are there in someone's time of financial need or even when a kindness might brighten another's day, it is more likely someone will be there in our time of need.

5. Circulate your treasures. I have had things in my life I really enjoyed. After a while they moved from the center of my life. I can store them hoping my interest will return. I can also find someone who may get as excited as I was about my former treasure. Their joy in receiving it brings me the joy of sharing in their pleasure.

A SOUL MATE REDISCOVERED

Soul mate is a term used fairly frequently these days. It can refer to a friend, a spouse or possibly a combination of the two. Some people talk about finding a soul mate to marry. Others find out their closest friend may be their soul mate. Although the term is becoming more common, I am not sure many people really stop to think about what it means. Souls are not much of a topic of general conversation lately.

Western philosophical and religious traditions have viewed the soul as the life force or principle and the center of thought, feeling and decision making. Many religious traditions understand the soul as living on independently of the body after death.

Looking at the soul in this way, a soul mate is a person in tune with our soul. More specifically a soul mate understands what we are thinking, what we are feeling and what our decisions are based on. When we are confused about our life direction, a soul mate can be there as a beacon to guide us back to ourselves and our life path.

Soul mates are not chosen out of a lineup. They seem to drift into our lives like other acquaintances, but as time goes by, they gct to know us at least as well as we know ourselves. They don't necessarily agree with everything in our lives, but they do understand what we are about. It is very comforting to know someone else thoroughly understands us and knows what our life is about.

I had a soul mate enter my life in 1959 before I had ever heard of the word. He was there with me for all of my decisions, troubles and joys. Even if I did not see him for some time, we did keep in touch. When we got together, it was as if we just saw each other yesterday. We could pick up right where we left off.

We suddenly lost track of each other in 1982, neither of us knowing what became of the other or how to get in contact. I often thought about him over the years, wishing he were there to understand what I was going through in tough times and to share my joy in good times.

We rediscovered each other a little while ago and we have been in almost daily contact since then, mostly catching up on what happened since we last saw each other and how our common experiences left their mark on us. I still feel that he understands me, where I have been and where I am headed, better than anyone else I know. I feel like a part of me has been restored and that I again have my soul mate with me in my life adventures.

Are you lucky enough to have a soul mate in your life? If so, cherish him or her and value your closeness as you would part of yourself. I have learned the value of my soul mate through the years of his absence. Welcome back Gerry.

A LETTER TO MY GRANDSON

Dear Joey,

I thought about using your formal name, but this is how my Uncle Fred started his letter to me when I was born fifty-nine years ago. Of course, I could not read the letter then, but I have gotten it out from time to time over the years. When I was born, the world was in the middle of a war involving most of the large countries. Fortunately that ended. We have had some smaller wars over the years. Two years ago, we started a new millennium and every-one hoped for a new beginning with peace in the world. Unfortunately it has remained easier for people to hate than to love each other.

I thought about this yesterday when you were born. You were surrounded by love all day long. You were the most beautiful boy I have ever seen, and the most peaceful, at least until you got hungry.

All of the people who love you have gone through hard times which I will let them tell you about when the time comes. All of them have worked hard to be at peace and to have love fill their hearts, which they now share with you.

I know your mother has worked hard to be at peace and will have much to teach you about how to be successful in life. Your father will be able to teach you the joy of music, which has often brought peace to my heart. Your sister jumped for joy when you were born and will be there to show you the ropes as you grow up. Like your sister, your brother had the unusual privilege of participating in your parents' wedding and I am sure he will be there when-ever you need him. When you are growing up, brothers and sisters can sometimes seem like a pain. As you get older, you will come to appreciate them and find out they really care about you if you let them become part of your life.

There are many other people who love and care about you, some your relatives, and some friends of your parents. If I could have one wish for you, it would be that you would always be surrounded by the love I saw around you yesterday and that those of us who love you could protect you from the hard times which all of us eventually grow through. I know the hardest thing for me as a parent has been to watch my children struggle with hard things in their lives, especially when I did not know how to help them. I do know it is easier to get through hard times when you know you are loved. It is quite clear that you are well loved. We will all do our best to love you no matter what you have to face in life. I hope all of us who love you now can be there for you whenever you need us.

Love,

Grandpa Joe

DEAR LOVED ONE

Dear Loved One,

I continue to be tortured by the mental illness which locks you in its embrace. It makes me very sad to see what it has done and continues to do to you.

When you were born, you seemed anxious to get out of the womb and get on with life. You were always quite enthusiastic about everything you did and approached each new adventure giving it your all. I still remember the picture I took of you running through a field holding up a daisy as if you were the first one ever to discover one. I will never forget your joy at that moment, or my own.

You went off to school as another new adventure, but very quickly found that sitting still was beyond your capacity and contrary to your adventurous spirit. You were on the go constantly until your body finally wore out and you needed rest. Do you remember the picture of you, asleep in the closet, sugar cubes in one hand and hugging the beagle with the other hand?

Reading seemed a daunting task for you and school was a struggle for years. Getting up to face the frustration of another day sitting at a desk was frequently more than you could manage.

After years of frustration, you finally learned in high school that you had a great talent for art and received a national gold medal for your first major piece. I was never more proud of you and thought your life had turned around.

The remainder of school was still quite a struggle. After you graduated, I was quite surprised to see you get up at five in the morning to go to work each day. Although your work did not focus entirely on your art, you did continue with it, to my constant delight in each new piece you created.

Your ambush by mental illness has been the hardest thing I have had to face in my life and still brings tears to my eyes. I think of all the talent you have within you and your struggle each day to pull yourself out of the swamp of mental illness just to survive. I shudder to see the tremor in your hand caused by your medication, knowing you have to choose between creativity and sanity. I want you to be whole again, to use your creativity and to be happy. I am very saddened to see you on the edge of despair and feel helpless to be of any assistance to you.

You feel stuck in your situation, and don't see any way out. I could tell you that things can get better, but I know it is hard for you to believe me. This is something you have to learn on your own when you are ready. I know how hard it is to cling to the slim thread of promise when everything around you feels like quicksand.

I want you to know I have faith in you and am praying and hoping for the day when you will be able to find yourself again.

COPING WITH A FRIEND'S ILLNESS

Somehow we always expect close friends to be there for us and we to be there for them. We are usually thinking of things we or they can do to solve an immediate problem. But what if the problem has no immediate solution?

I have a friend who has become quite close to me over the past few years. Due to the distance between us, we do not see each other often. We usually get together once a year in the summer or fall. When we are together, we can talk openly about any topics, no matter how personal. I suppose I take him for granted most of the year, although we do talk on the phone from time to time.

I called him yesterday just to say I loved him. It turned out he was suffering from Charcot syndrome, degeneration of bone tissue in the foot. Surgery to correct the condition led to an infection further complicated by his diabetes and associated circulatory difficulty.

He has always been a very active, free spirit and has enjoyed exploring new places as well as hidden aspects of familiar ones, such as New Orleans. Now, he is not able to maintain his own house and has to depend on relatives for his daily existence, not even able to walk. As a result, he has become quite depressed about his limitations.

My first reaction was a feeling of helplessness. I realized there was nothing I could do to make his foot better. There was nothing I could do to restore his independence. All I could think of to do at the moment was to tell him how sorry I was that he was going through this ordeal. I tried to imagine what I would do in his situation and thought of spending more time reading all the books I never seem to have time for. However his diabetes has also affected his eyesight, making it hard for him to read, so that would not be an option for him.

I have learned in my lifetime that every adversity leads to an opportunity if I remain open to it. But it is easier to understand this when the opportunity arrives than it is in the throes of adversity. It seemed cruel to tell him something good will come of his loss of independence, the one thing which mean so much to him. I will discuss this with him when I think he is ready to hear it, although I don't think that time has come yet. It will be up to him to find a way to cope with this turn of events in his own way. I don't think it is my job as a friend to tell him how he should approach it. I see my job as keeping alert to signs that he is ready to start adapting to his new circumstances and then being there for him in whatever way I can. Godspeed, Michael.

SUGGESTED READINGS

Beattie, Melody. *Codependent No More: How to Stop Controlling Others and Start Caring for Yourself.* Hazelden, 1997.

Beattie, Melody. *The Language of Letting Go.* Hazelden, 1996.

Bradshaw, John. *Healing the Shame that Binds You.* Health Communications, 1988.

Butterworth, Eric. *Spiritual Economics: The Principles and Process of True Prosperity.* Unity, 1988.

Cameron, Julia. *The Artist's Way.* Tarcher/Putnam, 1992.

Goleman, Daniel. *Emotional Intelligence.* Bantam, 1995.

Hanson, Peter. *Stress for Success: How to Make Stress on the Job Work For You.* Doubleday, 1989.

Haley, Jay. *Uncommon Therapy: The Psychiatric Technique of Milton Erickson.* Norton, 1993.

Hill, Napoleon. *Think and Grow Rich.* Fawcett Crest, 1960.

Kinney, Jean and Leaton, Gwen, *Loosening the Grip* (5th Edition) Mosby, 1995.

Lessor, Elizabeth. *The New American Spirituality: A Seeker's Guide.* Random House, 1999.

Moore, Thomas. *Care of the Soul.* Harper Perennial, 1994.

Moore, Thomas. *Soul Mates.* Harper Perennial, 1994.

Peters, Tom. *In Search of Excellence*. Warner, 1988.

Ponder, Susan. *The Dynamic Laws of Prosperity*. Devorss, 1962.

Ruiz, Don Miguel. *The Four Agreements*. Amber Atlas, 1997.

Selye, Hans. *The Stress of Life*. McGraw Hill, 1956.

Thoreau, Henry David. *Walden*. Houghten Mifflin, 1995.

Zukav, Gary. *The Seat of the Soul*. Simon and Schuster, 1990.